MW00669288

The Rural Primitive
in American
Popular Culture

Studies in Urban–Rural Dynamics

Series Editors: Gregory M. Fulkerson and Alexander R. Thomas,
SUNY Oneonta

This series focuses attention on understanding theoretically and historically the development and maintenance of Urban–Rural Systems through a spatial, demographic, and ecological perspective. It seeks a blending or reintegration of the urban, rural, and environmental research literatures under a comprehensive theoretical paradigm. As such, we further specify Urban–Rural Dynamics as analysis of human population distribution on social variables, including politics, economics, and culture.

Recent Titles in Series

The Rural Primitive in American Popular Culture

All Too Familiar

Karen E. Hayden

LEXINGTON BOOKS
Lanham • Boulder • New York • London

Published by Lexington Books
An imprint of The Rowman & Littlefield Publishing Group, Inc.
4301 Forbes Boulevard, Suite 200, Lanham, Maryland 20706
www.rowman.com

6 Tinworth Street, London SE11 5AL, United Kingdom

Copyright © 2021 The Rowman & Littlefield Publishing Group, Inc.

All rights reserved. No part of this book may be reproduced in any form or by any electronic or mechanical means, including information storage and retrieval systems, without written permission from the publisher, except by a reviewer who may quote passages in a review.

British Library Cataloguing in Publication Information Available
ISBN: 9781498547604 (cloth) | ISBN: 9781498547628 (pbk)

Library of Congress Control Number: 2020947239

∞™ The paper used in this publication meets the minimum requirements of American National Standard for Information Sciences—Permanence of Paper for Printed Library Materials, ANSI/NISO Z39.48-1992.

For all my rural relatives, past and present.

Contents

Preface and Acknowledgments

Growing up in a rural region of New Hampshire, in a town where both my mother and father grew up, and where my father's father also grew up, I wondered why people from certain towns were viewed as "inbred" and "lawless," but the people in my town were not. Living on a road where my last name appeared on three mailboxes within an eighth of a mile of each other, and where my oldest brother added his own house and mailbox, I questioned why and how certain common family names in some close-knit communities came to signify both inbrededness and the town itself; but not so in my town. My town and its inhabitants did not become a defining space, a place marking those born into it. My town does not shadow the perceptions of those who pass through it and live near it. This book grew out of my curiosity about why some rural people and places are viewed as too tight-knit, too close, and all too familiar. Because of this curiosity, I have honed in on themes of rural others in popular culture and found the notion of the rural primitive to be a very hearty and enduring stereotype—so enduring that I view it as a mythology. The mythology involves both positive (rural as bucolic) and negative (rural as horrific) ideas about rural life, but I am drawn to the more grotesque views of rurality because they exist at an almost subconscious level in American popular thinking and they dehumanize rural people. I hope this book sheds light on this myth-making and offers a way to critique assumptions about people who are viewed as living on the rural margins of an increasingly urban society.

I would like to thank all of the people who helped me work through this book. I am lucky to be a part of a small community of rural thinkers—scholars who grapple with rurality and what it means in a world that is increasingly biased toward urban and away from rural. My thanks to Alex Thomas and Greg Fulkerson, both at SUNY Oneonta. Their dedication to rural scholarship is nothing short of remarkable, and I appreciate being a part of it. Thanks to Leanne Avery and Brian Lowe, also at SUNY Oneonta. Thanks also to Amy Viera at Norwich University and Karl Jicha at North Carolina State University. A special thanks to Stephanie Bennett at the College of Saint Rose, who reviewed the book—I am very grateful for your kind words. I would also like to give a shout-out to rural criminology scholars whose ideas and critical perspectives are a welcome turn within criminology. Joseph Donnermeyer and Walter DeKeseredy's enthusiasm for rural criminology is contagious and helped me to think through many of the issues discussed in this book. And I will always be thankful to Mike Brown of Northeastern University for being such a positive and critical influence in my academic life.

Thank you to Courtney Morales at Lexington Books: you are a perfect mixture of support and gentle nudges when needed. I hope we can work together again. And thank you to Lexington Books for allowing me to include versions of material that was published previously in Fulkerson and Thomas's *Studies in Urbanormativity: Rural Community n Urban Society* (2014) and Fulkerson and Thomas's *Reimagining Rural: Urbanormative Portrayals of Rural Life* (2016).

I lucked out in the family department, and I want to thank them. Thank you to Mark Kelley, always. Thank you to my daughter, Evelyn Hayden Kelley, for being an astute reader, sounding board, and movie buff. It is a pleasure to watch you become a writer. Thank you, Kathy Hayden, for your enduring support. I am so glad we can lean on each other. Thank you to my brothers Mike and Pete and of course my parents, James E. Hayden and Carole Mahoney Hayden.

Chapter 1

Introduction

The Rural Primitive in American Popular Culture

When did rural, poor whites begin to be associated with inbreeding, primitivism, and violence and viewed as *other*—as less than, or even as scary? In this book, I look at how the mythology of the inbred, primitive rural became linked to evolutionary theories, both biological and social, that emerged in the mid-nineteenth century. The rural primitive fit well onto an imaginary continuum of primitive to civilized, rural to urbanormative, backward- to forward-thinking, and regress versus progress. The seeds of this mythology can be found even earlier in U.S. history—as early as the colonial period when white-indentured servants were brought to colonial America as laborers who made the so-called new world possible (Isenberg, 2016). In each chapter of this book, I use popular cultural depictions of the rural primitive to illustrate the ways in which this trope was used to set poor, rural whites apart from others. Not only were they set apart, they were also set farther down on the imaginary continuum of progress. Outsiders viewed them through a prism of what they lacked—no property, no work ethic, no morals. They were defined by what they were not: as "un"—uncouth, uncivilized, unfit.

Certainly, the seeds of this rural primitive notion existed before social theorists such as Herbert Spencer put it to use in social Darwinist conceptions of an evolutionary march toward progress with primitivism at the opposing end of a spectrum reaching toward civilization. Historian Nancy Isenberg traces the idea of "poor white trash" as far back as America itself. As she illustrates, "waste men" and "waste women" were the landless indentured servants who served the earliest colonists (Isenberg, 2016, p. 42). The colonists' interest in this class of people grew when they started reproducing—having "waste children" who could also be exploited for cheap labor (Isenberg, 2016, p. 42). Keeping them property-less insured that they would be a readily available

1

Figure 1.1   Photograph of a Rural West Virginia Landscape by Elizabeth Pell.
Source: **Used with the artist's permission.**

laboring class to work the land of the colonizers. The social mobility of this
group would not serve the needs of those in power. As Isenberg states,

> The rural poor, though seen as a liability, became an unbanishable part of
> the American experience. . . . Land was the principal source of wealth. . . .
> Hereditary titles may have gradually disappeared, but large land grants and land
> titles remained central to the American system of privilege. When it came to
> common impressions of the despised lower class, The New World was not new
> at all. (2016, p. 63)

Thus, the notion of a group of poor whites mired in their lower station in life
was useful to even the earliest American colonists. Not only did they have a
group of laborers at the ready, when slavery replaced indentured labor, they
also had a constant reminder of how much better they were than the poor
whites who were cast as lazy, shiftless, idle, and responsible for their own
poverty.

In the mid- to late 1700s, commentators on land disputes in the Wyoming
Valley and historians of Georgia's gold rush used the now-familiar terms of
"brutish," "lawless," and "backward" to describe the locals they encountered
(Stewart, 2011). In the late 1700s, travel writers moving north through the

Appalachian region described the locals as physically, socially, and economically backward, as prone to violence, and as animal-like (Stewart, 2011). If you look carefully, you can see such terms running through various forms of popular culture up to the present day.

I explore depictions of rural communities and rural places in American popular culture, focusing on the mid-nineteenth century to the present. I examine what I call the mythology of inbrededness that is attached to many rural locales. I locate this myth-making within the larger notions of degeneration, devolution, and primitiveness that emerged in nineteenth-century America. How did these poor, rural whites, previously viewed as trash and as mired in the dirt, become recast as the primitive point of a pseudoscientific spectrum marking the early stages of evolutionary progression? The mythology of inbrededness—a fusion of folk wisdom with the language of degeneration—took hold in the 1800s with the advent of Darwin's theory of evolution and its many misuses and partial understandings. I examine how the idea that inbreeding leads to degeneration and primitivism has been used, reused, and incorporated into American popular culture through stories, jokes, put-downs, folklore, and horror films. Degeneration and beliefs about inbreeding provide a context for the interpretation of situations and a text for speculation. I investigate the popular imagery of rural, insular, and supposedly inbred communities and how these types of places and people became a cautionary tale.

In 1893, French social theorist Emile Durkheim wrote of small, rural, agricultural communities: "What brings men together are mechanical causes and impulsive forces, such as affinity of blood, attachment to the same soil, ancestral worship, community of habits, etc. It is only on these bases that cooperation is organized" ([1933] 1964). In 2020, American popular culture stigmatizes and demeans these very same community features as backward, as anti-modern, and as downright scary. On television and movie screens, affinity by blood and ancestral worship become overly related, inbred families who attack outsiders. Attachment to the soil is portrayed as creepy monsters springing forth from the ground—as if the people and the scary rural landscapes are one and the same. And impulsive forces rule these primitive people's lives as they resort to brutal killings, cannibalism, and, always, inbreeding.

Criminologists and sociologists use the terms "collective efficacy" and "social integration" to describe rural communities as places where common values, mutual trust, and informal social control enhance social relations and keep citizens in check (Rogers and Pridemore, 2016). Collective efficacy is viewed as a positive attribute of rural communities; it typically stands in contrast to urban areas' perceived social disorganization and its attendant residential instability, crime, and juvenile delinquency. The idea of the rural primitive represents the dark side of social integration. These places and people possess too much integration, too much commonality. How was this positive attribute reconfigured as a negative? Isn't tight-knittedness something communities should want to cultivate?

I argue that small, rural, tight-knit communities, where "everyone knows everyone" and "everyone is related" came to be, for those on the outside, an allegory for what will happen if society, or even small segments of society, resist modernization, urbanization, and association with others in the steady march of progress. The message of the inbred community is clear: degeneracy, primitivism, savagery, regression, lawlessness, and an overall devolution will result if groups are allowed to become too insular, too close, *too familiar.* For the mythology of inbrededness to become so entrenched and unassailable, it needed to creep into the popular culture of the mid- to late nineteenth century. The mythology grew so potent and enduring because it has been continuously recreated over time, resulting in a type of taken-for-granted, mundane knowledge permeating everything from schoolyard ridicule to horror stories. These larger cultural messages in turn inculcated the image of reputed inbred towns or places and locked them into their roles as regional examples of a larger cultural bogeyman which we all fear, or at least keep at arms' length. Such places become readily available receptacles for a cultural lesson that we as a society feel the need to learn and relearn.

In each chapter, I look at examples of how this image of rural primitivism has been continuously reinvigorated in American popular culture. I examine rural depictions and stereotypes found in several forums, such as social Darwinian-laced appeals to change cousin marriage laws in the 1800s and how those messages made their way into eugenics campaigns that existed well into the early 1900s; redneck jokes and white trash stereotypes found throughout the mid- to late 1900s; and horror films of the late 1900s—when the terms "backwoods horror films" and "hillbilly slasher" entered the popular vocabulary and inbred monsters lodged in the popular imagination. I continue this line of exploration into twentieth-century backwoods horror films that have carried the inbred mythology through to the present day. I also consider how the rural-as-scary aesthetic of these horror films, a part of the rural primitive notion, has now made its way into true crime television where it becomes a daily reminder of those frightening others—the rural primitives in our midst.

The idea of the rural primitive taps into the larger mythology of degeneration that stands as an alternative myth to the tale of progress, of moving forward. The specter of primitive types nearby hints at the dark side of progress. The notion of primitivism tied to inbreeding is seen as particularly insidious as it is a corruption by blood—an irreversible decline. It is a secular, genetic fall from grace to replace previously intact religious falls from grace.

Stereotypes of rural people as either (1) simple, village folk who still live in a romanticized, pastoral idyll; or (2) inbred, cannibalistic monsters hinder meaningful knowledge and understanding of the lived experiences of rural people. These two opposing images stand as urbanormative ends on a continuum of oversimplifications of rurality. Both forms of othering allow outsiders to disregard rural people and to view them as not fully human. Their exploitation by the coal industry, paper mills, or fishing or logging industries is not an issue. Their back-breaking labor in the factory farm/meat-packing industrial complex remains hidden. The lack of health care in rural parts of the United States is not a concern. Real victims of rural crime do not register—crimes take place in urban areas, right? Rural people only appear in the media as curiosities or monstrosities, so why should we be concerned about their intergenerational poverty? Further, long-standing stereotypes of rural people dictate that they bring these misfortunes on themselves because they are lazy, because they won't pull themselves up out of the dirt or mud or swamps they are mired in, or worse yet, because they inbreed.

I focus specifically on the mythology that has been built up around rural people and places and look for ways in which the mythology can be dismantled, or at least called into question using critical sociological and criminological perspectives. I look specifically at notions of inbreeding, which have not received a thoroughgoing examination outside of scientific or pseudoscientific discourses. A few recent academic studies have started to explore rural horror films, but they have not connected these popular cultural media to earlier narratives that used the same mythology of inbreeding in other forms of storytelling. I connect these seemingly disparate cultural dots.

In chapter 2, "Inbreeding, Cousin Marriage and the Rural Primitive in Nineteenth-Century America," I explore how the equation of consanguinity to degeneracy was loosely modeled on nascent nineteenth-century bioevolutionary paradigms exemplified by Darwinism and Herbert Spencer's social evolution. Consanguinity is the practice of marrying within a small group of related people. The more popular term for this marriage and sexual practice was "inbreeding," which was inexorably linked to devolution, degradation, and degeneracy. Further, inbreeding became inextricably tied to the idea of a rural primitive. Consanguinity was the purview of royals and landed gentry who kept both their relatives and their fortunes close, but inbreeding became the practice of rural people who didn't know any better. I examine how inbreeding is defined and perceived in different eras and how it is justified by reference to historically specific cultural themes and according to different figures of speech. I also consider where and when inbreeding is tolerated under special circumstances pertaining to relative class, status, and power. The questions of when is inbreeding looked upon disparagingly and when is it deemed appropriate or permissible are central to this chapter.

In chapter 3, "Inbred Horror and the Rural Primitive in Twentieth–Century Popular Culture," I look at how urbanormativity grows out of a popular culture that distorts rural reality and contributes to the idea that urban is the way forward and rural is the way backward. Ideas about what is normal, acceptable, and desirable possess an inherently urban characterization. Rural itself has come to be defined as different, as deviant, as other. I continue to examine the mythology of inbrededness and where it fits within the larger nineteenth-century idea of degeneration and the rural primitive. I illustrate that rurality and tight-knittedness came to represent a cautionary tale: society must move forward, people must progress toward urban, civilized life. In the urban-rural divide and cultural ideal of urbanormativity, the message of the inbred community is clear: degeneracy, primitivism, savagery, regression, and an overall devolution will result if groups are allowed to become too insular and closed off to the outside world.

For the evolutionary schema to become so entrenched and unassailable, it needed to creep into the popular culture of the mid- to late nineteenth century and be continuously recreated over time, resulting in a type of taken-for-granted, mundane knowledge. Inbred place myths and rural primitives become perennial examples of a cultural lesson that we, as a society, feel the need to learn and relearn. I examine depictions of inbred communities in popular culture and the language, metaphors, and discursive practices of these cautionary tales. I illuminate how and why rural, inbred people and places became such a powerful image, and why they remain so.

Chapter 4, "Inbred Horror Revisited: The Rural Primitive in Twenty-First-Century Backwoods Horror Films," extends the analysis of the rural primitive and its association with inbreeding and degeneracy to its recent manifestations in backwoods horror films. By closely examining this rural cultural bogeymen—and they are almost always men—I provide a more nuanced understanding of how social representations of the rural primitive have become increasingly skewed and distant from reality while reinforcing urban life as a normal state of affairs. The stock image of scary, inbred rural folk has become such an identifiable characterization in movies that backwoods horror films, also known as hillbilly horror/slasher and even inbred movies, are now recognized as a genre unto themselves. In this chapter, I investigate the backwoods horror movie genre at the turn of the twenty-first century to see what these stories tell their viewers about rurality.

I expand this analysis to a different medium in chapter 5, "*Murder Comes to Town*: The Rural Primitive on True Crime Television." Like the rural-themed backwoods horror films, rural crime on true crime television perpetuates ideas about rural places as dark, sinister, and *scary*. Specifically, I discuss rural true crime storytelling on Investigation Discovery (ID). An examination of ID's substantial true crime offerings reveals that many of its original programs feature violent crimes that take place in small-town and rural settings. Shows with titles such as *Murder in the Heartland, Killing Fields, Murder Comes to Town, Welcome to Murdertown, Fear Thy Neighbor, Dead North*, and *Swamp Murders* are a few of the many rural-themed offerings on ID. The names themselves evoke far-off locales where few dare to tread. Similar to the imagery found in backwoods horror movies, the shows' lead-ins, promos, and other visuals showcase dark, spooky forest scenes, run-down houses nestled in wooded lots, weathered barns and sheds, rusted silos and farm equipment, barbed wire fences, and lonely dirt roads. These types of images make up what I call the rural-as-scary aesthetic, following my examination of backwoods horror movies, as well as the work of Fulkerson and Lowe (2016), who examined representations of rurality in popular U.S. television shows from the 1950s to present. Their analysis found that the predominant television characterization of rural is one of "morally dangerous, negative, and implicitly inferior" people and places (Fulkerson and Lowe, 2016, p. 32). I explore these urbanormative assumptions in a new venue for the rural-as-scary aesthetic: rural true crime.

In chapter 6, "Not So Familiar: Thinking Beyond Rural Stereotypes," I consider how knowledge and understanding of rural people and places are hindered by the stereotypes of rural people perpetuated in popular culture either as simple village folk who still live in a romanticized, pastoral idyll or as inbred, monstrous, cannibalistic maniacs as represented in backwoods horror films. These two opposing images—both inherently primitive—can be seen as counterpoints on a continuum of oversimplifications of rural people. Both forms of othering allow urban outsiders to disregard rural people and the challenges they face. In this concluding chapter I ask: Can we talk about the rural in popular culture without talking about rural stereotypes? I explore recent rural representations in American popular culture to see where rural people are portrayed in a more nuanced, thoughtful manner—as antidotes to the rural stereotypes discussed in previous chapters of this book.

Since rural primitive stereotypes have served to divide people across racial lines, class lines, and regional lines, I consider who benefits from these divisions. I also stress the importance of questioning poor, white, rural stereotypes when they appear in discussions of rural crime. While Hollywood continues to make and remake movies about inbred rural cannibals, and true crime television shines a bright light on a handful of rural people's worst days, rural inhabitants of the United States are both victims and perpetrators of real crimes—domestic violence, arson, burglaries of farm equipment, drug abuse, such as oxycodone, which began as a rural drug problem and spread into cities and suburbs and is now linked to the heroin abuse plaguing the United States. Further, people from rural regions also work in some of the most physically taxing and unsafe jobs: farming, logging, and mining, to name just a few. In many of these dangerous jobs, workers are unprotected from the demands of industry owners and shareholders who view labor as a renewable resource and not as human lives. And rural regions bear a disproportionate amount of damage from environmental crimes such as the discharge of contaminated water from the coal industry, from the extraction of (fracking) natural gas, and from meat processing plants. Rural crimes are very real, but they do not involve scary inbred monsters; they are perpetrated by wealthy industry owners who may have never stepped foot on the soil they contaminate or seen the water they spoil.

Crime is just one of the many social problems found in rural places throughout the country, the same places that have been described for centuries as pockets of rural primitivism. Recent writings in rural studies, including those featured in this series, Urban-Rural Dynamics, take up the task of offering more critical perspectives on rural issues. In the final chapter of *The Rural Primitive in American Popular Culture: All Too Familiar*, I explore contemporary rural representations in American popular culture to see where rural people are portrayed in a more nuanced, thoughtful manner. The critically acclaimed film *Winter's Bone* (2010) offers one such example of a rural suspense-drama that is neither romanticized nor horrific. The story focuses on Ree, played by Jennifer Lawrence, a teenage girl trying to keep her family together in the face of extreme poverty in the very rural Ozarks. The movie paints an unromantic, realistic portrait of a strong female protagonist who is neither the victim nor the perpetrator of a bloody crime. She and her family survive through her strength and grit. I explore this film and other correctives to the rural stereotypes found in popular culture of the late twentieth to early twenty-first centuries to find cultural examples of areas within popular culture that offer more careful, thoughtful examples of rurality.

Chapter 2

Inbreeding, Cousin Marriage, and the Rural Primitive in Nineteenth-Century America

The equation of consanguinity, or marrying within a small group of related people, signifying degeneracy was loosely modeled on the nascent nineteenth-century bio-evolutionary paradigm exemplified by Darwinism and Herbert Spencer's social evolution. Inbreeding and its links to degradation and degeneracy are the topics of this chapter. I focus on inbreeding, or the marriage and/or procreation of close kin, in the United States from the mid-nineteenth century to the present. I consider how inbreeding is viewed in different historical periods and how it is sometimes disparaged and other times seen as unproblematic and even sensible.

While the term "inbreeding" implies incestuous relations, I limit my discussion to marriage and procreation between cousins and other non-immediate kin members. I do not directly address incest between immediate or nuclear family relatives, such as father and daughter or brother and sister incest. Since discussions and theories of inbreeding and incest are often intertwined, after first examining the meanings of the two terms, I try to single out, as much as possible, the specific discourses that apply to cousin marriages and other consanguineous unions. The reason for this limitation is my interest in inbred towns or inbred places where marriages to relatives have occurred, or are perceived to have occurred, at high rates. I am interested in communities that are seen as tightly integrated, almost tribal, due to the endogamous practice of marrying within a relatively small number of families.

I review the literature on inbreeding and cousin marriages from the historical period of the mid- to late nineteenth century. In doing so, I situate

Figure 2.1   Charles Darwin and Emma Wedgewood Darwin, Husband and Wife and First Cousins. *Source*: Images from Wiki Media Commons, Free Media Repository (https://commons.wikimedia.org).

the specific set of images defining rural poor people in a more established, general, eugenics-influenced discourse of progress and decline associated, at the turn of the century, with social evolution. My review of the literature on inbreeding and cousin marriage is by no means exhaustive. It is intended only to indicate structures of meaning and ideas that operate as resources in the development of rural primitive identities. I attempt to exclude discussions of father-daughter, mother-son, and sibling incest, since the notion of the inbred town tends to refer to a small number of families intermarrying within the community or township. Regardless of sexual relations among immediate family members (real or perceived), the negative image of inbreeding and degeneracy centers on a small number of interrelated families.

I confine my discussion to European-American kinship structures and the myths that attach to variations in kinship rules and norms and the reactions to deviance around that set of rules. Kinship structures and definitions of family are clearly social and cultural constructs. Marriage restrictions and bans on certain types of marital and sexual unions vary along with culturally constructed definitions (Levi-Strauss, 1969; Fox, 1983; Parsons and Bales, 1955). There is no single type of family within either the American or English contexts, though the nuclear family model is taken as typical, obligatory, and thus became hegemonic. This structure usually includes the father as the head of the household, mother, and children living under one roof. First cousins include children of the mother's or father's siblings. Cross cousins are, for example, daughters of mothers' brothers or of fathers' sister; parallel cousins are daughters of mothers' sisters or father's brothers (Ottenheimer, 1996; Gough, 1989). A functionalist version of the family unit stresses the division of labor necessary for successful socialization of children, with the father as instrumental and the mother as socio-emotional leader (Parson and Bales, 1955). This version treats variations in sexual unions as more or less dysfunctional to socialization.

INCEST AND INBREEDING

Incest is commonly understood to mean sexual relations between closely related family members. However, the degree of relatedness is not commonly understood, nor is the impetus behind the prohibition of such unions. The lack of agreement on these issues has been a common theme among anthropologists and sociologists for over a century (Arens, 1986). The incest taboo has often been called a universal taboo; however, its universality is open to debate. For instance, in *The Original Sin: Incest and Its Meaning*, Arens explores not only the incest prohibition but the deed itself (1986). He notes that when human beings "in any place or form, which may include the printed word in our time, reflect upon the incest taboo, they are confronting a theme commonly believed to represent a baseline in the definition of morality" but that "the matter has not been resolved to everyone's satisfaction" (Arens, 1986, p. ix). Arens contends that because of linguistic variations in the meaning of both the terms "incest" and "taboo," these prohibitions are far from universal. For instance, the English term "incest" derives from the Latin *castum*, meaning chaste—connoting purity—whereas incest equals impurity. But in Germanic languages, the term involves the notion of "blood shame." In Chinese the word for incest connotes disorder, and in Indonesian the term is related to repugnance (Arens, 1986, pp. 5–6). In other societies, there is a lack of explicit concepts around the topic of incest, but there are behavioral rules that exclude the activity nonetheless. Still, other societies have no "apparent past or present experience with the behavior" and thus no uniform response to its violations (Arens, 1986, p. 6).

Further, the term "taboo" can mean different things to different groups. In English, it was borrowed from the Polynesian language of Tonga, and it is not an absolute prohibition. Instead, its original meaning was "acts set apart or consecrated to a special purpose; restricted to the use of a god, king, or chiefs, while forbidden from general use" (Arens, 1986, pp. 6–7). However, in modern English usage, it has come to be synonymous with "prohibition."

Neither the incest taboo nor the act of incest is universal—the "very concept is culture-bound. . . . To view it as universal is to sweep away crucial complexities" (Arens, 1986, pp. 5–7).

Theories of incest and its prohibition have been put forth throughout history in various disciplines ranging from religion and theology to social anthropology, sociology, psychology, ethology, psychoanalysis, biology, and sociobiology. A full review of the literature on the incest taboo and various theories of incest avoidance and prohibitions have been undertaken elsewhere (see Arens, 1986; Degler, 1991; Hertier, 1982; Fox, 1980). The theories explaining the incest taboo have ranged from religious doctrines that view marriage and sexual relations with kin members as wicked and evil to sociobiological theories that contend that humans have an innate aversion to incest. Alliance theories and structural functionalist paradigms argue that the incest taboo and exogamy, or marriage outside one's group, are the very basis for society. Groups forged alliances between and among themselves when men exchanged women from within their groups for marriage to men from outside groups (Levi-Strauss, 1969). Alliance theory is attributed to the French structural functionalist Claude Levi-Strauss, who said, "The incest prohibition and exogamy have an essentially positive function . . . the reason for their existence is to establish a tie between men which the latter cannot do without if they are to raise themselves from a biological to a social organism" (1969, p. 493). Levi-Strauss believed that the incest taboo and exogamous marriage practices marked human progress from primal nature to social structure and culture.

The idea that exogamy builds and strengthens social ties and political alliances was not a new one; it had been put forth by much earlier theorists, including the fourth-century Catholic philosopher Saint Augustine (Ottenheimer, 1996). In the late nineteenth century, the English evolutionist Sir Edward Tylor (1878, 1881) developed the basic principles of alliance theory by broadening the concepts of endogamy and exogamy first put forth by the Scottish theorist, John Ferguson McLennan (1865). Tylor's research greatly influenced Levi-Strauss's studies on kinship forms.

A more recent scholar of incest, W. Arens believes that despite both our natural and cultural disinclinations toward incest, some humans do indeed commit the act (1986). In a reversal of Levi-Strauss, Arens believes that incest itself, and not its absence or prohibition, is what sets humans apart from other animals (Arens, 1986; Degler, 1991). Following a sociobiological argument, he states that "the source of the aversion to the familiar partners is an innate proclivity, while the prohibition of others as sexual or marriage partners is social or cultural in origin" (Arens, 1986, p. 99). This belief leads him to remark, "in a convoluted way, nature is responsible for a rule prohibiting incest, in an equally complex fashion, culture is responsible for its appearance in human affairs" (1986, p. 156). Thus, in Arens's line of argument, it is people's capacity to *ignore* a natural and cultural rule that marks humanity. The recent book by sociologist Gloria González-López, *Family Secrets (Secretos de Familias): Stories of Incest and Sexual Violence in Mexico* (2015), would seem to shore up Arens's line of reasoning. González-López illustrates that although Mexico is a largely Catholic country with sexual taboos of all kinds—including the incest taboo—yet incest between close and extended family members indeed occurs and is even built into the strict patriarchal norms of some family cultures.

Since I am primarily concerned with the theories that view marriage of kin members as leading to degeneracy, backwardness, and primitivism, I will move away from the vast theoretical debates over the incest taboo to focus on arguments against marriage and sexual relations among non-immediate kin members in the mid- to late nineteenth century in England and the United States. I will focus specifically on the field of evolution and how the rhetoric of this discipline made its way into American marriage laws through hygienic concerns over hereditary defects and fears of the weakening or degrading of human genes. I am also interested in how and why certain unions were constructed as problematic in the American context, but not necessarily so in England. Before discussing these developments, I will review the Judeo-Christian religious foundations for marriage laws in England and America. I then turn to a discussion of the legal changes that took place in the American forum.

LEVITICAL PROHIBITIONS OF CONSANGUINITY AND AFFINITY

The Roman Catholic Church was largely responsible for the prohibition of first cousin marriages in the West. In the eleventh century, the Catholic Church adopted the Germanic (or Canonic) method of calculating degrees of relatedness (Ottenheimer, 1996). This method increased the range of prohibited filial kin, and within the Germanic proscription, relatives as distant as sixth cousins were forbidden from marrying unless they were granted a dispensation from the church (Ottenheimer, 1996). Church scholars disagree as to why cousins were not allowed to wed under Roman Catholicism, but some theorize that the prohibition allowed the church to gain monetarily by disrupting traditional patterns of familial inheritance and the continuity of European family estates (Goody, 1983; Ottenheimer, 1996). While it is not clear how forbidding cousins to marry channeled money into the church, the proscriptions had a latent effect. Because the degrees of relatedness were so extensive in the Germanic method of reckoning, many couples used it to dissolve unhappy marriages. Because divorce was difficult to obtain under the rules of the church, many people who were unhappy with their marriages delved into their family genealogies to find proof that the marriages were incestuous to begin with and thus had to be dissolved. Particularly among the aristocracies, genealogical evidence of "some sort of dubious relationship" (Duby, 1983, p. 173) could usually be found, and where it was not found, it could be fabricated. A cottage industry of genealogical researchers and paid witnesses grew up around the new forbidden marriages. Because the Germanic method of determining kinship was used to end marriages, and thus posed a threat to family stability, in 1215, forbidden degrees were lessened to third cousins or closer collateral relatives (Ottenheimer, 1996).

According to Ottenheimer, the issue of kinship restrictions on marriage played a role in the sixteenth-century revolt against the church by Martin Luther, and the Protestant Reformation of the sixteenth century did away with such prohibitions (Ottenheimer, 1996, 1990). Since the Protestant Reformation, most European countries have not included cousins in laws prohibiting marriages between relatives, and none do today (Ottenheimer, 1996). While the Anglican Church forbade certain familial unions on the grounds that they were immoral and disruptive to family stability, first cousins were not prohibited from marrying. The various denominations of Protestantism in America held differing beliefs about cousin marriages. Most often, they were either accepted or opposed but not forbidden.

Kin marriage restrictions in Anglo-American civil law date back to medieval canonical law and its "forbidden degrees" (Grossberg, 1985; Wolfram, 1987; Ottenheimer, 1996). Like other marital restrictions, marriage laws concerning consanguinity, people related by blood, and affinity, people already related through marital ties, were influenced by the biblical admonitions in the Old Testament's book of Leviticus, Chapters Eighteen and Twenty (Grossberg, 1985; Wolfram, 1987; Anderson, 1986). For instance, in Chapter Eighteen, "Unlawful Marriages and Unlawful Lusts," Number Six states, "None of you shall approach to any that is near kin to him, to uncover *their* nakedness: I *am* the Lord." Numbers Seven through Twenty-One specify the degrees of relatedness more explicitly; however, first cousins are not one of the prohibited degrees (*The Holy Bible, Old and New Testaments*, 1868. The Harding Royal Edition). The prohibited acts, as well as those of adultery, homosexuality, and bestiality, were considered immoral and wicked and transgressors were threatened with the punishment of being "cut off from among their people" and/or expelled or "spued [*sic*] out of the nations" (Lev. 18:29).

The prohibitions in Leviticus Chapter Twenty, "Of Adultery and Of Incest" were similar in their degrees of relatedness, but called for more severe punishments; for instance, "If a man lie with his daughter-in-law, both of them will surely be put to death: they have wrought confusion, their blood shall be upon them" (Lev. 20:12). This particular passage reveals why these relations were seen as wicked—they create *confusion*. Other words used to describe these pairings are iniquity, meaning wickedness, but also connotes unevenness, uncleanliness, or a basic lack of order.

Mary Douglas examined Levitical prohibitions in *Purity and Danger* (1966). Douglas confines her Levitical examination mainly to food restrictions, but her analysis of Leviticus is useful in understanding just what these proscriptions protected—why they were considered polluting sins. Douglas also discusses the Levitical concerns with order and notes that anything that connoted mixing or confusion was forbidden (1966). Order and completeness exemplified holiness, and holiness requires that *"different classes of things shall not be confused"* (p. 53, emphasis added). Douglas also contends that "under this head all the rules of sexual morality exemplify the holy. Incest and adultery (Lev. 18:6–20) are against holiness, in the simple sense of right order . . . holiness is more a matter of separating that which should be separated than of protecting the rights of husbands and brothers" (1966, pp. 54–55). However, here Douglas seems to be dodging the question of *why* is morality and holiness a matter of stating who should and not marry and/or have sexual relations, or why *some* unions are moral and others are not. The issue of what is potentially confused is not answered satisfactorily.

What exactly is protected from confusion? It would be easy to assume that familial relations are confused and chaos over who occupies what role in the family will ensue if already related people are allowed to marry and have children. However, this is not an obvious statement, since Douglas confines most of her discussion to the mixing *outside* of categories as dangerous and confusing to wholeness and completeness. It does not automatically follow that mixing within categories, or families, is a threat to completeness and order. In fact, one could argue just the opposite—that to stay within family categories is to stave off the confusion of strangeness and unfamiliarity. Indeed, Douglas states, "Other precepts extend holiness to species and categories. Hybrids and other confusions are abominated" (p. 54).

Similarly, Christie-Davies (1982) studied other Levitical prohibitions, such as taboos against homosexuality, bestiality, and transvestism (Lev. 18:22–24; 20:13–14). He argued that these strict prohibitions served to fortify social boundaries between groups and strengthen in-group solidarity, particularly when there was an external threat (1982). While Davies's exclusion of the incest taboo in his analysis is a notable omission, he clearly reinforces the notion that Levitical rules of conduct are concerned with *separation from* other groups—of creating and maintaining *distinctions*. He states, "These rules confer no possible economic, medical, or demographic advantage on the people who keep them. Imposing a ban on the breeding of that invaluable but sterile hybrid the mule must have been a serious handicap for an agricultural people" (1982, p. 1034). Davies's analysis provides many examples of how *difference itself* is perceived as threatening. The need to make distinctions as clear as possible—of man versus beast, of the living versus the dead, of male versus female—underpins his interpretation of Leviticus. So, why would it follow that marriage and sexual relations of kin members—among those within the group—are restricted? Perhaps this is why Davies left the incest taboo and kin marriage proscriptions out of his analysis; he leaves unanswered the question of why something that could further shore up in-group boundaries and keep others apart is prohibited. If the book of Leviticus is so preoccupied with distinctions to the point of warning off hybridization, it seems a strange place to include in-group marriage proscriptions. Something appears to be missing from both Douglas's and Davies's interpretations of Levitical abominations. So, what, then, would be confused if certain types of intrafamilial unions were not prohibited?

Returning to Douglas's *Purity and Danger*, in a later chapter, she makes the argument that the boundaries of the body symbolize the boundaries of society (1966). She asserts:

> The idea of society is a powerful image. It is potent in its own right to control or to stir men to action. This image has form; it has external boundaries, margins, internal structure. Its outlines contain power to reward conformity and repulse attack. There is energy in its margins and unstructured areas. For symbols of society, any human experience of structures, margins or boundaries is ready to hand. (p. 115)

Thus, if marriage and procreation within a family represent a confusion not just of family roles but also of *bodies*—individual bodies—perhaps this is what is protected. The sharing of bodies in incestuous unions must be prohibited because it threatens the external margins of the self, the corporeal individual. For instance, Douglas discusses Jean-Paul Sartre's use of stickiness or viscosity to illustrate one way in which human beings are capable of confronting anomaly. Viscosity is repellent because it blurs the essential relation between the subjective experience and the outside world. Describing a child plunging its hand into honey, Douglas says,

> Its stickiness is a trap, it clings like a leech; it attacks the boundary between myself and it. . . . Plunging into water gives a different impression. I remain solid, but to touch stickiness is to risk *diluting myself into viscosity*. Stickiness is clinging, like a too-possessive dog or mistress. In this way the first contact with stickiness enriches a child's experience. He has learnt something about himself and the properties of matter and the interrelation between the self and other things. (1966, pp. 38–39, emphasis added)

Douglas, following Sartre, argues that melting, clinging viscosity is judged as an "ignoble form of existence in its very first manifestations" (1966, p. 39). What might Douglas's discussion of the margins of the body and Sartre's viscosity tell us about early Levitical prohibitions against marriages of too-close kin? Perhaps what is muddied or confused in close relatives involved in sexual relations—and thus possibly procreating—are the individual bodies themselves. A blurring of bodies and an undeveloped notion of the individual margins of selves could result. This would present a confusion much more damning than unclear familial roles. The following statement from Douglas furthers this point:

> Sexual collaboration is by nature fertile, constructive, the common basis for social life. But sometimes we forget that instead of dependence and harmony, sexual institutions express rigid separation and violent antagonism. So far, we have expressed a kind of sex pollution which expresses a desire to keep the body (physical and social) intact. . . . Another kind of sex pollution arises from the desire to keep straight the internal lines of the social system . . . we noted how rules control individual contacts which destroy these lines, adulteries, incests and forth. (1996, p. 141)

Here, Douglas again discusses the need to keep sexual lines of contact straight both from within and outside the social system. Further, since Douglas has used the body as a metaphor for the social system itself, it follows that certain sexual unions within the internal lines of the system would lead to the confusion of bodies, the smallest divisible internal system. This confusion would in turn cause chaos in the entire system.

In the following section of this chapter, I discuss how these Levitical admonitions were codified into canonical law and subsequently into English and American marriage laws. I consider the differences within and between the laws in these two settings and the controversies they stirred.

MARRIAGE PROHIBITIONS:
ENGLAND AND THE UNITED STATES

In the early history of England, marriage fell under ecclesiastical control. As previously discussed, canon law, following Leviticus, was the original source of rules forbidding related people from marrying. Previous to the period of Henry VIII, "disqualifications because of relationship had been extended beyond all reasonable limits" (Vernier, 1931, p. 173; see also Wolfram, 1987; Anderson, 1986). During Henry VIII's reign, 1491–1547, the government passed a statute that "forbade the ecclesiastical courts from invalidating any marriage unless the parties were more closely related than first cousins" (Vernier, 1931, p. 173). Thereafter, English law forbade a man from marrying his mother, sister, grandmother, father's or mother's sister, daughter, or granddaughter, and the same degrees applied to a woman. Further, under the English doctrine, "a man was considered to be related by blood to all the blood relatives of his wife, and the wife to those of the husband" (Vernier, 1931, p. 173). Thus, the same prohibited degrees applied to those related by affinity.

In America, legal marriage prohibitions of people already related through blood, marriage, or adoption can be found in every state. As Vernier, an early nineteenth-century scholar of American family law, notes,

> From earliest times in history of marital institutions the marriage of persons related within certain degrees, whether by consanguinity or by affinity, has been prohibited. There has been no complete agreement upon the extent to which the prohibition of marriage on account of relationship shall be carried, and in modern times, especially, there has been much argument whether or not relationship by affinity ought to be a ground for prohibiting marriage at all. This tendency is revealed in the United States, where such marriages are prohibited in only half the states. (1931, p. 173)

Similarly, marital law scholars William J. O'Donnell and David A. Jones state:

> Proscriptive rules of one sort or another can be found in every jurisdiction, although variations exist in the types of relationships enjoined. First-cousin unions, for instance, are classic examples of marriages that may or may not be recognized, depending on the jurisdiction involved. . . . The major functional concerns behind these injunctions are two: the fear that incestuous dyads increase the risk of genetic-defect transmission and the fear that such dyads jeopardize family equanimity and stability. States accordingly raise these concerns, together or separately, by way of denying various candidates the fundamental right to marry. (1982, p. 50)

Martin Ottenheimer's book *Forbidden Relatives: The American Myth of Cousin Marriage* (1996) brings to light the provisionality of these laws and the question of how close is too close concerning kin marriage in the United States. He states in his introduction, "The American myth of cousin marriage . . . first appeared in the United States over two hundred years ago. Beginning in the middle of the nineteenth century it found its way into our legislation system, and a majority of states passed laws against first cousins marriage that remain on the books to this day. Almost invariably, challenging this myth evinces a strong emotional reaction among Americans" (1996, p. 2).

In the American context, prior to the middle of the nineteenth century, cousin marriage was a common convention, and only a handful of states had laws forbidding it (Ottenheimer, 1996, 1990). Historian Daniel Scott Smith noted that, particularly in the New England states, there was a "distinctively high level of kinship density in early America" (1989, p. 44). Smith's quantitative analysis of surnames in a sample of early New England federal censuses indicated that up until at least 1790, many inhabitants of New England towns were "all in some degree related to each other" (1989, p. 44). However, by the latter part of the nineteenth century, over 60 percent of states had laws prohibiting first cousin marriages. For instance, the state of New Hampshire was one of the first to enact laws prohibiting first cousins from marrying. In 1869, New Hampshire changed its general statutes relating to marriage. Prior to this time, New Hampshire had governed marriages under the 1695 Massachusetts act that stated that no man could marry his father's sister, mother's sister, father's widow, wife's mother, daughter, wife's daughter, son's widow, sister, son's daughter, daughter's daughter, son's son's widow, brother's daughter, or sister's daughter. The corresponding relatives were prohibited for women (*The Revised Statutes, State of New Hampshire*, 1842). In 1869, New Hampshire added that "no man shall marry his father's brother's daughter, mother's brother's daughter, father's sister's daughter, or mother's sister's daughter (*Laws of the State of New Hampshire* 1867–1871). Previous marriages that fell within the prohibited degrees were declared "absolutely void without legal process" (Vernier, 1931, p. 179).

New Hampshire's early adoption of cousin marriage laws is particularly notable since several New England states never adopted such laws at all. Massachusetts, Connecticut, Rhode Island, and Vermont still legally permit first cousin marriages. Until 1985, Maine had no law prohibiting cousin marriage, but adopted one at this time "under supposition that it would prevent birth defects in offspring" (Ottenheimer, 1996, p. 25). In 1987, the Maine legislature permitted cousins to marry only if they could provide the town clerk with certification from a physician that they had had genetic counseling. Maine is the only state with any such genetic counseling provision, though other states permit cousins to marry if one of the partners is sterile (i.e., Illinois) or if one or both of the partners are beyond a certain age (i.e., sixty-five in Arizona or fifty-five in Illinois) (Ottenheimer, 1987). These exceptions reveal that the impetus behind cousin marriage laws in the United States was clearly a matter of procreation and the supposed detrimental effects to the offspring of such unions.

During the same historical period in Europe, no country legislated against first cousin marriage, and cousins are still legally permitted to marry in every country in Europe (Ottenheimer, 1996, 1990; Anderson, 1986). In examining what accounts for the sudden shift in laws in the United States, and the absence of laws prohibiting marriages of cousins in Europe, the debate over inbreeding in the two contexts becomes clearly demarcated along the lines of church and state and the newly forming fields of evolutionary biology and its effects on the social sciences.

THE NINETEENTH CENTURY: INBREEDING AND THE CULTURAL CLIMATE

As the review of Levitical admonitions demonstrates, the various arguments against incest in general and discussions about cousin marriages, in particular, had been the dominion of religion and belief systems until the mid-nineteenth century. However, as "progress was the religion of the nineteenth century" (Pick, 1989, p. 2), the field of expertise changed and marriage laws became the purview of new scientific discourses of evolution and medicine. Martin Ottenheimer found the shift against cousin marriage in the United States was justified largely by reference to evolutionary anthropology and evolutionary biology. Two major figures in each field, Lewis Henry Morgan, an evolutionary anthropologist, and Charles Darwin, an evolutionary biologist, had married cousins. Darwin was also the child of a cousin marriage. Darwin's case illustrates how common this practice was among members of the upper classes of Victorian England (Anderson, 1986). One part of the story of consanguinity and incest is how the debates around the topic varied by class status (Ottenheimer, 1996; Anderson, 1986).

Lewis Henry Morgan

American anthropologist Lewis Henry Morgan's wife and cousin, Mary Elizabeth Steele, was active in the Presbyterian Church in Rochester, New York. The minister of this church, Joshua McIlvaine, was strongly opposed to cousin marriages and spoke against it at a literary club to which Lewis Henry Morgan belonged. Though they were close friends, McIlvaine did not dissuade Morgan from marrying his cousin, nor did he prohibit the marriage from taking place. At the time, Morgan's own views on the subject had not yet been transformed. Further, the Presbyterian Church in the United States did not approve of cousin marriage but had no rules in place to prohibit them (Ottenheimer, 1996, 1990).

Lewis Henry Morgan's marriage exemplifies how readily America adopted the evolutionary schema in reference to marriage laws. When Morgan married his cousin in the state of New York in 1851, there were no laws prohibiting the union. In fact, unlike the majority of states in the United States, to this day, New York has not adopted laws against cousin marriages (Ottenheimer, 1990). However, within only a few years, Morgan had changed his mind about such marriages, stating in his major work, *Ancient Society*, that "as intermarriage within the gens was prohibited, it withdrew its members from the evils of consanguine marriages and thus tended to increase the vigor of the stock" ([1877] 1963, p. 68). Morgan's reference to both "the evils" and "vigor of stock" in the same sentence highlights the intermingling of moral, religious warnings with nascent evolutionary notions that were by no means clearly articulated nor empirically tested. What, after all, is "the vigor of stock," and how is it related to evil? Morgan cannot help us here. In England and the United States, after the middle of the nineteenth century, religious justifications for marriage restrictions increasingly overlapped with—and were eventually displaced by—references to evolution, but with differing effects. The perceived deleterious hereditary effects of consanguineous procreation became the focus rather than discussions of wickedness, sin, and disruptions of the family that prevailed in the religious tenets.

CONSANGUINITY AND EVOLUTIONARY "PROGRESS"

Richard Hofstadter, a foremost scholar on social Darwinism in the United States, argued that because evolutionary ideas have become so ingrained in American ideology, we tend to forget just how wide-sweeping Darwin's theories were and are. Hofstadter states:

> Mankind has lived so long under the brilliant light of evolutionary science that we tend to take its insights for granted. . . . Many scientific discoveries affect ways of living more profoundly than evolution; but none have had a greater impact on ways of thinking and believing. . . . Indeed, there have been only a few scientific theories whose intellectual consequences have gone far beyond the internal development of science as a system of knowledge to revolutionize the *fundamental patterns of thought*. (Hofstadter, 1969, pp. 1–3, emphasis added)

In considering the shift in American attitudes about consanguineous marriages, several important scientific developments must be considered. The first is Darwinian evolutionary theory and its popularization in America.

The second—intrinsically related—field is social evolutionary theory, social Darwinism. The strongest proponent of social Darwinism was the English theorist, Herbert Spencer, who traveled to the United States in the mid-nineteenth century as a guest of Andrew Carnegie, steel tycoon and philanthropist (Hofstadter, 1969). Spencer coined the phrase "survival of the fittest" and was concerned with mental evolution more so than physical evolution. The third development was within the field of medicine, or what Lawrence Grossberg (1985) termed "the hygienic invasion of marriage law," wherein the newly formed, mid- to late nineteenth-century scientific discourses were brought to bear on marital unions by translating "fears of hereditary defects" into "more comprehensive nuptial codes bringing all possible family members within the incest ban" (Grossberg, 1985, p. 140).

Evolutionary Theory

In his book *Social Darwinism in American Thought*, Richard Hofstadter points out: "England gave Darwin to the world, but the United States gave to Darwinism an unusually quick and sympathetic reception . . . thinkers of the Darwinian era seized upon the new theory and attempted to sound its meaning for several social disciplines" (1969, pp. 4–5). Darwin's *The Origin of Species* was first published in America in 1860, and from that point on, popular magazines such as *Appleton's Journal*, *Popular Science Monthly*, and *The Atlantic Monthly*, as well as daily newspapers, published articles on natural selection and Darwinism (Hofstadter, 1969). The language of evolution, of progress and natural selection, and Herbert Spencer's adage "survival of the fittest" propagated in subjects "quite remote from science" and became "a standard feature of the [American] folklore of individualism" (Hofstadter, 1969, pp. 3–4, 50).

Simultaneously, in American anthropology, evolutionary theorists like Lewis Henry Morgan observed consanguineous marriages among some Native American groups as well as other indigenous groups around the globe (Morgan, [1862] 1959; Ottenheimer, 1990). Morgan's evolutionary framework purported that such kin marriages were incompatible with the process of evolution, and therefore must be seen as a stage that "had to be surpassed in order to be civilized" (Ottenheimer, 1990; see also Boehrer, 1992). For instance, in his *Ancient Society: Researches in the Lines of Human Progress from Savagery through Barbarism to Civilization*, Morgan writes of the consanguine family, stating, "As the first and foremost ancient form of the institution, it has ceased to exist even among the lowest tribes of savages. It belongs to a condition of society out of which *the least advanced portion of the human race emerged.* . . . It . . . has outlived for unnumbered centuries the marriage customs in which it originated" ([1877] 1963, p. 410, emphasis added). From the evolutionary point of view, then prevailing, kin marriages were backward, regressive. Morgan's entire body of work was an attempt to map out human evolution through an examination of family and marriage forms. In 1877, he wrote the following ode to exogamy:

> The influence of this new practice, which brought unrelated persons into the marriage relation, must have given a remarkable impulse to society. It tended to create a more vigorous stock physically and mentally. . . . When two advancing tribes, with strong mental and physical characters, are brought together and blended into one people by accidents of barbarous life, the new skull and the new brain would widen and lengthen to the sum of the capabilities of both. Such a stock would be an improvement upon both, and this superiority would assert itself in an increase in intelligence and numbers. ([1877] 1959, p. 468)

It's hard to not be persuaded by such a romantic image of these accidental unions; however, Morgan overlooks the fact that in America—his model for advanced societies—very clear anti-miscegenation laws in many states prohibited the marital joining of certain groups within our own borders. Presumably, those were not the skull and brain combinations he had in mind. Morgan makes many contradictions and murky assumptions in his theories, not the least of which is the fact that while he posits his convictions in favor of exogamy, he himself was married to his cousin. He explained his own cousin marriage by saying that since he married a *cross cousin* (his mother's brother's daughter), this was qualitatively different from a *parallel cousin*, at least in his own framework. He argued that the "crucial factor in the emergence of exogamy is the avoidance of intermarriage within the 'gens' of consanguineous families. . . . In the unilineal descent systems these kinds of marriages are exogamous" (Ottenheimer, 1996, p. 111). Thus, in his own theory, he viewed his marriage as neither endogamous nor primitive. However, the distinction between cross and parallel cousins was not made in any of the newly forming laws against cousin marriage in the United States. These new laws were emerging at around the same time as the publication of his *Ancient Society.*

One of Morgan's more problematical assumptions was the notion that in the first stage of his evolutionary framework, primitive humans had indiscriminate sex with relatives and whomever. This evolutionary stage was never discovered by Morgan; he simply constructed it as the beginning point in his evolutionary framework. The idea of the promiscuous horde was disputed by other evolutionary theorists of the day, most notably by Darwin himself, who wrote in *The Descent of Man*, "[I] cannot believe that absolutely promiscuous intercourse prevailed in times past, shortly before man attained his present rank on the evolutionary scale" ([1874] 1901, p. 759).

Nonetheless, Morgan's view of the progression of marriage types became widely accepted in America. In *Ancient Society*, Morgan displayed his "overriding assumption that some societies, including our own, had progressed through earlier arrangements, while others still maintained their more primitive expression due to their lower position on the evolutionary scale" (Arens, 1986, p. 30). Further, Morgan believed that these remaining societies provided a "living history of social forms which he believed could still be charted in the present" (Arens, 1986, p. 30). Morgan viewed human groups as a living, breathing cabinet of curiosities that could be arranged from bottom shelf (unevolved inbreeders) to top (evolved outbreeders).

Through Morgan's evolutionary notions, first published in 1877, but undoubtedly circulating in the years prior, we can begin to see how ideas about pockets of primitivism in the midst of civilized society emerged. But, in order for these ideas to take their shape in legal prohibitions, they also had to be linked with other prevailing views of the day.

Spencerian Social Evolution

Lewis Henry Morgan's theory of the stage-like progression of family forms from primitive to civilized was but one of the many evolutionary frameworks advanced in the mid- to late nineteenth century. Though quite influential—he is sometimes called the "father of American anthropology"—but so is Franz Boas—Morgan did not single-handedly change American ways of thinking about evolution and marriage patterns. A fundamental notion of nineteenth-century evolutionary theory was that the earliest peoples lived in "undifferentiated groups, without recognizing kinship ties, without marital prohibitions, and without rules governing sexual conduct" (Ottenheimer, 1996, p. 105). The English social theorist Herbert Spencer also believed that such "primitive hordes" marked early societies and that human evolution was a process of specialization, differentiation, and increased complexity.

Spencer, while interested in population issues, did not specifically take up the issue of marriage laws in England or the United States. But, as Hofstadter notes, his philosophies were "admirably suited to the American scene" (1969, p. 31) and influential in many American arenas, including sociology, business, biology, politics, and government. In coining the phrase "survival of the fittest," Spencer was concerned with mental, intellectual evolution. He thought that if mental characteristics could be inherited, "the intellectual powers of the race would become cumulatively greater, and overall the ideal man would finally develop" (Hofstadter, 1969, p. 39). He saw the poor as categorically unfit and opposed any aid to them since they should be eliminated through natural selection. Andrew Carnegie, who brought Spencer to America and became his close friend, added to Spencer's theory by stating,

"Man was not created with an instinct for his own degradation, but from the lowest he has risen to the higher forms" (quoted in Hofstadter, 1969, p. 45). Spencer also purported that some American settlers were becoming savage-like, and the country itself was at risk for regression to savagery. He said in 1851, "The back settlers, amongst whom unavenged murders, rifle duels, and Lynch Law prevail—or, better still—the trappers, who leading a savage life have descended to savage habits, to scalping, and occasionally even to cannibalism—sufficiently exemplify it" (quoted in Ottenheimer, 1996, p. 114). By Spencer's colorful descriptions, these different American types would no doubt fit nicely into Henry Lewis Morgan's living history of social forms.

The "Hygienic Invasion of Marriage Laws"

The predominance of evolutionary theory in the mid-nineteenth century to the turn of the twentieth century provided a powerful backdrop for concerns about "regression," "backwardness," "primitivism," and "savagery." However, for these new scientific frameworks to affect marriage laws, they also had to be cast as a public health danger and legal issue. As Michael Grossberg noted in his examination of nineteenth-century family laws, *Governing the Hearth*, "only extremely potent prejudices could dislodge the commitment to individual choice embedded in . . . American marriage law" (1985, p. 144). Hence, the evolutionary schema became interwoven with the emerging "hygienic invasion of marriage laws" that linked incest and inbreeding with newly forming biological and hereditary fears of degeneracy (Grossberg, 1985; Arens, 1986). The fear was that in the midst of all this progress, there could indeed be its opposite—regression, devolution, and throwbacks to a previous state (Greenslade, 1994). Where some social evolutionists such as Spencer thought that nature should be allowed to take its course unimpeded by any sort of state intervention; others disagreed. At the turn of the century, Darwin's evolutionary theory was utilized by social reformers who thought hereditary traits should fall within the purview of formal social control. The most obvious manifestation of this belief was the eugenics movement. Hofstadter writes:

> The theory of natural selection, which assumed that the transmission of parental variations, had greatly stimulated the study of heredity. Popular credulity about the scope and variety of heredity traits had been almost boundless. Darwin's cousin, Francis Galton, had laid the foundation of the eugenics movement and coined its name when Darwin was being sold to the public. In the United States, Richard Dugdale had published in 1877 his study of the Jukes, which . . . offered support to the common view that disease, pauperism, and immorality are largely controlled by inheritance. (1969, p. 161)

Galton's first writings on heredity were published in the late 1860s to 1880s, but the eugenics movement did not begin in earnest in the United States until the turn of the century. The hereditarian paradigm also contributed to changes in cousin marriage laws in the United States. As Ottenheimer observed, "The passage of laws against cousin marriage in a number of states in the nineteenth and early twentieth century was one of the several reactions to the fear that American society might degenerate" (1996, p. 114).

Typical American anti-cousin marriage sentiments are articulated in the following passage from Joel P. Bishop, a nineteenth-century scholar of U.S. marriage laws. In an 1852 volume of his treatise on marriage laws, he stated:

> Marriages between persons closely allied in blood are apt to produce an offspring feeble in body, and tending toward insanity in mind. They are everywhere prohibited; but the more common reason assigned for the prohibition is, that the toleration of it in families would impair the quiet of families, jeopardize the female chastity, and hinder the formation of favorable alliances. (quoted in Grossberg, 1985, p. 145)

In an attempt to shore up arguments for which social evolution had provided a backdrop, proponents of cousin marriage prohibitions tapped into these hygienic concerns and contended that inbreeding caused mental and physical weaknesses, such as feeblemindedness, insanity, and infertility. Other physical and mental deformities attributed to cousin marriage were dwarfism, cretinism, idiocy, insanity, epilepsy, deaf-mutism, sterility, rickets, and leprosy (Ottenheimer, 1996, p. 86). However, the evidence for these physical and mental deformities was scarce, and one 1870s researcher found no data to support these various health claims (Huth, 1875, p. 308).

The evolutionary proponents had their detractors, and many medical professionals found no evidence to support the degeneracy arguments. These opponents held that any unwanted physical or mental characteristics in offspring of cousin marriages were due to the *transmission* of the characteristics and not due to the genes *degenerating* (Ottenheimer, 1990). Thus there was, nor is, no conclusive scientific data to indicate that genes are *weakened* or *degraded* in inbreeding, but rather that the likelihood of the transmission of recessive genetic problems, such as deafness, will be heightened if both the maternal and paternal sides carry genes for deafness. The potential of similar recessive genes being transmitted to offspring *increases* in cousin marriage and procreation, but the *weakening* or *degenerating* of genes was not considered scientific fact by many professionals of the day (e.g., New York Medical Society of 1869, cited in Ottenheimer, 1990). Thus, neither Morgan's reference to increased or decreased "vigor of stock" (1877, p. 68) nor Bishop's use of "feeble offspring" could be verified any more than could earlier references to "evils" or "sins."

Despite the lack of definitive biological evidence on the dangers of cousin marriages, legal prohibition of these types of consanguineous unions increased steadily in the United States after the mid-1800s, and today about 60 percent of states prohibit first cousin marriages (Vernier, 1931; Ottenheimer, 1990). While concerns regarding affinal unions ebbed, the "longstanding antipathy to consanguineous unions revived and expanded as biological fears intensified . . . legislative attempts to ban those kin marriages that seemed the most threatening led to greater statutory uniformity" (Grossberg, 1985, p. 145). Both Ottenheimer and Grossberg attribute these changes in marriage laws to wider cultural changes in the United States beginning around the middle of the nineteenth century, namely the wide-ranging acceptance of the bio-evolutionary model and its emphasis on equating physical and mental characteristics in cousin marriages with degeneracy and primitiveness. Grossberg notes that an "increasingly cautious and often repressive legal environment gave way to 'social darwinism and scientific fatalism'" (1985, p. 145). The new inclination in civil marriage laws was to "take no chances with heredity" (Grossberg, 1985, p. 145).

Both Grossberg and Ottenheimer fail to discuss *why* the hygienic and bio-evolutionary proponents' claims were so persuasive in the United States, especially given the fact that the same evolutionary theories were present in England and other parts of Europe, yet they did not change marriage laws in any country in Europe. And the scientific data for the deleterious effects of inbreeding were not overwhelming. Morgan and his American audience may have been moved by his studies of Native North American groups in particular. The need to separate the European colonizer from the colonized Native Americans could well have been an impetus for America's rush to adopt the bio-evolutionary model in marriage laws, since, at the same time, English Parliament refused to adopt such laws. As Richard Parker argued in *Bodies, Pleasure, and Passions* (1991), the sexual practices of the colonized are often used as a means to create the "savage other" in the process of colonization. Similarly, Christie-Davies noted that taboos against certain sexual practices, such as bestiality, homosexuality, and transvestism, have long been wielded as instruments to establish, maintain, and defend social boundaries (1982, pp. 1032–1063). The image of "primordial incestuous promiscuity," while not proven to have existed, is a powerful way to set one group off from a supposedly more advanced, intelligent, and highly evolved group. The imaginations of the colonizers, fueled by new scientific terminologies of, on the evolutionary side, "primitiveness" and "regression," and, on the bio-genetic side, "degeneration," "feeble bodies," or "feeblemindedness" fortified their preexisting beliefs. The absence of any clear incest taboo, references to inbreeding, lack of distinct family roles, and ignorance of who belongs to whom are very useful tools in the creation of barbarous, savage others in need of colonization (Parker, 1991, pp. 12–13).

Ottenheimer suggests that in England, despite the presence of Darwin and other evolutionists, there was less widespread acceptance of the bio-evolutionary model and the changing of marriage laws. Here again, Ottenheimer stops short of any real conclusions on this difference between England and the United States, but I believe property considerations may have had much to do with England's hesitance in forbidding first cousin marriages. Thus, while several U.S. states were adopting legal prohibitions to close-kin marriages because of its territorial need to separate the colonizers from the "primitive" Native Americans, English Parliament actively resisted such legal prohibitions because cousin marriage served the purpose of keeping property and wealth within the upper and aristocratic classes.

Nancy Fix Anderson's study of cousin marriage in Victorian England, while not discussing property considerations directly, does locate the propensity to marry first cousins in the middle and upper classes of Victorian England. Both Ottenheimer and Anderson show that, as with their American counterparts, English evolutionary theorists of the mid- to late nineteenth century were hotly debating consanguineous marriages and procreation (Anderson, 1986; Ottenheimer, 1996; see also Wolfram, 1987). Darwin himself, who was both the product of cousin marriage and married his first cousin, and had children in the marriage, nonetheless believed that inbreeding was harmful not just because it *intensified* existing genetic traits but that it *caused* degeneracy (Anderson, 1986; Ottenheimer, 1996, p. 85). Darwin only briefly mentioned his belief that marriage and procreation of close relatives are injurious to offspring in his first edition of the book, *Various Contrivances by Which Orchids are Fertilized* (1871). By 1877, in a later edition of the book, he changed his views and affirmed that cousin marriage does *not* represent any evolutionary risk. This conclusion was drawn after his son, George Darwin (who clearly had reason for concern), had undertaken a study of consanguineous unions in England and found no genetic risks to offspring (Ottenheimer, 1996).

The evolutionary theories did spark some apprehension in England, however. Some members of the English Parliament wanted to ask census questions about cousin marriages to determine if there were any detrimental effects to offspring in first cousin unions. Many debates ensued, ranging from those who objected to cousin marriage to proponents of eugenics who were diametrically opposed to the idea of prohibiting cousin marriage and used arguments of "purity of stock" as their scientific evidence (Anderson, 1986). Despite the scientific and medical debates of the day, unlike many states in the United States, English Parliament did not seriously entertain the idea of legally prohibiting first cousin marriages (Anderson, 1986; Ottenheimer, 1996; Wolfram, 1987). Indeed, some members of Parliament in the late nineteenth century were so adamantly *against* laws prohibiting such consanguineal marriages that they wanted to ask the same census questions as their opponents in order to prove that there was no biological harm to the offspring of cousin marriages. In contrast to the United States, Wolfram notes that the major point of contention within English debates over marriage laws was that of an affinal relationship—of a man marrying his deceased wife's sister (1987).

While both Ottenheimer and Anderson stop short of examining property and economic interests in the legal debates about first cousin marriages, the connection between the integrative effects of consanguineal marriages in the formation and reproduction of aristocratic classes had been considered in both England (Trumbach, 1978; Boehrer, 1992) and the United States (Gough, 1989), as well as other regions (Arens, 1986; Twitchell, 1987; Raglan, 1991). In contrasting the class-based differences in views about incest and inbreeding in Renaissance England, Bruce Thomas Boehrer (1992) found:

> Incest in lower classes is seen as a function of living habits that held space and property in common. . . . Nothing could be farther from the truth when we come to the matter of royal/noble incest. In such cases, both as they appear in historical records and as they appear in literary figurations—incest is almost inseparable from the *accumulation* of property and privacy. It becomes, in short, an attribute to bourgeois existence, modeled on the prerogatives of the kingly nature. (p. 154)

This passage clearly illustrates the constructedness and provisionality of notions of incest and inbreeding and their intrinsic links to wealth and property. Even within the same historical period, while it is seen as kingly for an aristocrat to marry and procreate with his cousin, it is seen as savage and primitive for a peasant to do so.

In the United States, the emergence of a bio-evolutionary framework for understanding human history made cousin marriage a threat to the "civilized status of the country" (Ottenheimer, 1996, p. 115). Further, "laws forbidding first cousin marriage were thus passed to protect the status of American society" because inbreeding was equated with savagery and degeneracy (1996, p. 115). However, there appears to be a missing link since—as Ottenheimer himself illustrates—the same bio-evolutionary ingredients were in place in Europe and particularly in England. I believe this link is material. Because of America's unique status as colonizers in a system of internal colonialism, considerations specific to this setting explain why some states in this country were rushing to adopt cousin marriage proscriptions at a time when no other place in the world was.

First, there was a need to separate both from the "mother country" of England, *and* the indigenous groups who were portrayed as barbaric and less than human in the colonizer's genocidal campaigns to usurp land. Second, there was the compulsion to ensure that a new aristocracy was not allowed to form through cousin marriage alliances and property consolidation. Simultaneously, there was undoubtedly a powerful resistance to these marital prohibitions that asserted itself in some states, but not others. These considerations can also help to reveal why cousin marriage laws are not uniform from state-to-state, another question that Ottenheimer leaves unanswered. For instance, Massachusetts and some other New England states never adopted laws against cousin marriage. Several social historians have noted that in nineteenth-century Boston and Salem, Massachusetts, the wealthy merchant classes used cousin marriage to maintain and consolidate their wealth and to form tightly knit political alliances (Gough, 1989; Hall, 1977; Farber, 1972). The landed gentry of the colonial Chesapeake region also tended to follow a pattern of first cousin marriages similar to that of the British aristocracy (Kulikoff, 1976; Gough, 1989). Like Massachusetts, neither Maryland nor Virginia adopted cousin marriage laws. These states already had powerful elite groups in place; therefore, they were able to resist the trend in cousin marriage prohibitions. The new world bourgeoisie also escapes the damning labels of primitives and savages. In Boston, for instance, these inter-married elites became known as Boston Blue Bloods or Brahmins, both of which are veiled references to inbreeding and aristocracy. Yet they are not accompanied by the negative imagery reserved for poor, property-less groups who were thought to have inbred.

Levi-Strauss theorized that the incest taboo and exogamous practices stood as the very genesis of culture. Social relations and exchanges between and among groups began because of the prohibition of incest and breeding within the group. The exchange of virginal women to men from other groups guaranteed social ties, reciprocity, and political and economic alliances between and among groups (Levi-Strauss, 1969; Rubin, 1975).

If the converse is true, then the endogamous practice of inbreeding insures a group's cohesion, integration, unity, and homogeneity. While this practice is seen as permissible, economically shrewd, and even aristocratic among some groups, it is viewed as primitive, degenerate, and savage, among others. Property and class status determine which image becomes attached to which group, or which image is deployed against a group. If members of the landed gentry marry within the family, they are protecting their family's wealth. They construct marriage and property laws that allow them to reproduce their aristocratic status.

Those without property who are allowed to grow too tightly knit, too famil-iar—the clannish poor who have nothing to protect—become horrific. These groups are inevitably viewed as problems since the poor have been viewed, and are still viewed, as morally inferior and dangerous (Gans, 1995). As I discuss in chapter 3, the horrific image of inbred families and inbred commu-nities represents all that is anti-modern and anti-urbanormative: regression, primitivism, barbarism. Further, there is the specter of the clan—a group of people intimately connected through blood, chromosomes, and flesh. They are not perceived as individuals; they are too close in body and mind. We are less concerned with tightly knit American elite families—perhaps because they are beyond social control. What appears to us as horrific are those clannish groups at the other end of the socioeconomic spectrum—the scary, rural poor Appalachian boy and the sodomizing "mountain men" in *The Deliverance,* for instance. They have become recognizable types—inbred types: dangerous, degenerate, atavistic throwbacks in the steady march of evolutionary progress. The chapters that follow address this inbred image—the shocking notion of pockets of primitiveness in American popular culture.

Chapter 3

Inbred Horror and the Rural Primitive in Twentieth-Century Popular Culture[1]

In this chapter, I explore the notion of the inbred community and how rural people and places are depicted in popular culture as deviant and even horrific. I place what I call the mythology of inbrededness within the larger nine-teenth-century idea of degeneration. I argue that these small, rural, tight-knit communities, where "everyone knows everyone" and "everyone is related" came to be, for those on the outside, an allegory for what will happen if society, or even small segments of a society, resist modernization, urbanization, and association with others in the steady march of progress. In the urban-rural divide and cultural ideal of urbanormativity, the message of the inbred community is clear: degeneracy, primitivism, savagery, regression, and an overall devolution will result if groups are allowed to become too insular, too close, too familiar. It is tight-knittedness to a fault.

As I discussed in chapter 2, the equation of consanguinity, or marrying within a small group of related people, signifying degeneracy and primitivism was loosely modeled on the emerging nineteenth-century bio-evolutionary paradigm exemplified by Darwinism and Herbert Spencer's social evolution. In their introduction to a collection of essays on the intellectual history of the notion of degeneracy, J. Edward Chamberlin and Sander Gilman find that

> the word degeneration was itself a curious compound. First of all, it meant to lose the properties of a genus, to decline to a lower type . . . to dust, for instance, or to the behavior of beasts in the barnyard. . . . In addition, the idea of degenera-tion encouraged typological, just as much as it organized physical and biologi-cal, speculation; and in its more popular aspect it invited some very unscientific stereotyping. Finally, and for all its connection with *natural* phenomenon, its most powerful association was with something *unnatural*—when associated with desire or supernatural dread. (1985, p. ix, emphasis in original)

Figure 3.1 Screenshot of the House from the X-Files Episode "Home" (Season 4, Episode 2, first aired October 1996). *Source*: Photograph taken by author.

This chapter explores one example of this unnatural, unscientific stereotyping and how it was manifested in a supernatural dread that I am calling the mythology of the inbred community. I examine how the notion of inbreeding has been used, reused, reconstructed, and incorporated into regional cultures through jokes, put-downs, folklore, imaginary boundaries, and horror stories—and how these examples of a larger association of the mythology of inbrededness became part and parcel to the idea of the rural primitive. As Chamberlin and Gilman contend, "Degeneration provided a context for the interpretation of situations, and a text for speculation" (1985, p. ix). I investigate how this text for speculation was serviced in popular imagery of insular, reputedly inbred rural communities and how these types of places and people became a part of an "ingenious fusion of folk wisdom with the language of degeneration" (Greenslade 1994, p. 174). I explicate how the larger message of "inbreeding leads to degeneracy and primitivism" became part of American popular culture and how this mythology become a warning to us all and to what end.

For the evolutionary schema to become so entrenched and unassailable, it needed to creep into the popular culture of the mid- to late nineteenth century. It endures because it is continuously recreated over time, resulting in a type of taken-for-granted, mundane knowledge permeating everything from schoolyard ridicule to horror stories. These larger cultural messages in turn inculcate the image of allegedly inbred places and lock them into their roles as "inbred communities"—as regional examples of a larger cultural bogeyman which we all fear, or at least keep at arms' length. Inbred place myths become readily available receptacles for a cultural lesson that we, as a society, feel the need to learn and relearn (Hayden, 2016, 2014a,b).

In his inquiry into the theme of degeneracy in late nineteenth-century British novels, William Greenslade (1994) discusses the function of myth-making and scientific discourses of regression and degeneracy. Using Frank Kermode's (1967) distinction between myth and fiction, Greenslade states, "The mythic component of a concept and practice such as degeneration lies in . . . its constructedness" (Greenslade, 1994, p. 3). Kermode wrote, "Fictions are made for finding things out, and they change as the need for sense-making changes. Myths are the agents of stability; fictions are the agents of change" (1967, p. 39).

The myth of inbrededness and particularly the rural inbred community became one such agent of stability in the larger concept of degeneration. Chamberlin and Gilman argue that degeneration crystallized some perennial disagreements about the continuities and discontinuities of natural history. As we saw in chapter 2, the idea permeated various thought-processes "from biology and genetics to sociology and psychology to literature and the arts . . . but it also became an inevitable structure of reality, an indisputable fact" (Kermode, 1985, pp. ix–x).

The idea of the so-called inbred community achieved the permanence of an indisputable fact and an inevitable structure of reality. The specter of the inbred community—the very tight-knit and insular group of people in rural, backwoods, or out-of-the-way settings—took on the role as a local reminder of a message of urbanormativity we must all heed, namely, the message of progress or regress. I examine depictions of inbred communities in popular culture and the language, metaphors, and discursive practices of these cautionary tales. I illuminate how and why the inbred town became such a powerful image, and why it remains so today.

SHIRLEY JACKSON'S VISION OF NEW ENGLAND

The first examples of the larger cultural message of inbred communities as degenerate and primitive come from Shirley Jackson's short stories "The Lottery" and "The Summer People," written in 1948 and 1950, respectively. Jackson's most popular short story, "The Lottery," presents an allegory of small-town barbarism wherein village folks gather once a year for a ritualized stoning of an arbitrarily selected town inhabitant. The lesser-known story, "The Summer People," shares the theme of the tightly knit, insular New

England community, its oddities, and even its horrors. "The Summer People," however, makes explicit the subject of the perceived inbreeding within the town as an explanation for its insularity and degeneracy, a theme only implied in "The Lottery." In "The Summer People," the scene of inbred horror is set in the following passage:

> Physically, Mrs. Allison decided, as she always did when leaving the grocery store after one of her inconclusive conversations with Mr. Babcock, physically, Mr. Babcock could model for a statue of Daniel Webster, but mentally . . . it was horrible to think into what old New England Yankee stock had degenerated. She said as much to Mr. Allison when she got into her car, and he said, "It's generations of inbreeding. That and the bad land." (Jackson, 2017, p. 184)

The Allisons are "summer people," outsiders from New York who own a vacation home in a fictional New England town where they spend their summers every year. Since they are retired, they decide to remain at their cottage beyond Labor Day, as they have nothing to rush back home to. The natives of the town consider this an unacceptable intrusion; after all, even the most touristy of towns wants to resume their normal lives after Labor Day. Summer people are not supposed to stay beyond the permissible time allotted for summer, and because of their native inbrededness, the townsfolk retaliate, plotting revenge against these interlopers. In the course of the short story, the natives degenerate; they regress from mildly annoying the Allisons with their slowness and inconclusive conversations to absolutely terrorizing them. By the end of the story, the Allisons are holed up in their cottage with no kerosene nor mail from the outside world. The town folk, growing increasingly restless, refuse to deliver these services to non-natives after Labor Day. Their phone line has been severed and their car disabled. They are trapped, and at the end of the story, the two old people are huddled together in the darkness waiting for the degenerate, inbred, primitive locals to come get them.

Jackson's story relies on the validity of the idea that the inbred, insular town is inevitably degenerate and thus dangerous, primitive, and even horrific. Other than their inbrededness and territoriality, no explanation is given for the native's monstrous turn. They devolve into creatures of instinct, predators lashing out at those who dare encroach upon their place, their home. What appears serene and bucolic on the surface can turn horrific, predatory, and savage within a matter of a day.

Shirley Jackson was not a native of New England; she grew up in California and then moved to Rochester, New York, where she attended college. She transferred to Syracuse University, and after college, moved to Bennington,

Vermont, from New York City. She lived briefly in Connecticut before returning to Vermont (Westbrook, 1982). Jackson is clearly able to distance herself
from the so-called degenerated Yankees about whom she became famous for
writing. Jackson's writing often conveyed humankind's potential for evil and
cruelty. To embody this gothic view of humanity, she relies on grotesque imagery of communal closeness; the towns depicted in both "The Summer People"
and "The Lottery" reveal the horror within. Jackson's New England villagers
are frightening because of their odd solidarity and their primitive, supersti-
tious rituals. The natives in "The Summer People," in particular, possess the
ability to be normal and abnormal, primitive and modern. They maintain some
semblance of normalcy to a point. When outsiders threaten their insular and
sacred social unit, however, they regress to their degenerate, primitive ways.

Jackson's stories are very brief; the reader is not given much information
with which to judge these strange primitives, and thus, their superstitions and
automatic distrust of outsiders appear innate or natural—it springs forth from
their very constitution. In both "The Lottery" and "The Summer People,"
the lure of the rural idyll—of a pastoral village life where everyone knows
everyone—turns grotesque. These are inherently degenerative tales. In "The
Lottery," the conductors of the stoning rite are prominent members of the
town. As Perry D. Westbrook discussed in his book, *The New England Town
in Fact and Fiction* (1982), the unity of this town is not reassuring; it is scary.
Discussing "The Lottery," he finds,

> Frighteningly noticeable is the solidarity of the people—their sense of being a
> tightly knit, even sacred social unit—in the spirit of New England social cov-
> enant. The town is all-important; the individual must be ready to give his life for
> its well-being. The people gathered in the town green gossip and joke familiarly
> just as they would at a Fourth of July celebration or at a town meeting. The lot-
> tery is but an episode of their yearly routine, another occasion when people meet
> and strengthen the bonds that hold them together. (Westbrook, 1982, p. 231)

After writing "The Lottery," Jackson argued that it should not be seen as
applicable only to New England towns and people. She explained that she
wrote the story as an "allegory of innate and universal human viciousness,
stupidity, and credulity" (quoted in Westbrook, 1982, p. 232). According to
Jackson, we all contain the primitive within us. Perhaps it is just more easily
aroused in these savage, tribal, and rustic rural settings.

In "The Summer People," the theme of degeneration is made even more con-
spicuous. In Jackson's urbanormativity, because the natives are so insular to the
point of being inbred, they can quickly revert to their innate, savage tendencies
that bubble just below the surface of their seemingly normal countenances.
In both stories, the theme of the people being tied to the land— the town

itself—also makes them appear anachronistic and backward. These are people who have lived in the same spot for generations upon generations, since Daniel Webster walked among them. This rootedness in a place and solidarity to home and township, almost unheard of "in this day and age," is also portrayed as inherently anti-modern and regressive. The natives turn hideous when their land is encroached upon because they see it as ancestral and inborn; it belongs to them, and, quite naturally, it must be defended and kept within the group.

HOME AND FAMILY

A more recent inbred horror story with themes of extreme insularity, regression, primitivism, and ties to ancestral land appeared on television's popular series *The X-Files*. The science fiction/drama series, created by Chris Carter, ran on American television from 1993 to 2002. In an episode entitled "Home," which first aired in October of 1996, the show's protagonists, Agent Dana Scully and Agent Fox Mulder, find themselves investigating an inexplicable horror—not unusual for these two Federal Bureau of Investigation paranormal experts. Indeed, it is the basis for the so-called speculative fiction program (Genge, 1995). However, the horror in this particular episode was not the usual alien abduction, giant parasitic monster, or evil government conspiracy that Scully and Mulder typically find themselves chasing but never quite explaining. This episode is about a small, rural, and seemingly bucolic Mayberryesque town and a family known as the Peacocks.

The program begins with the wails of a child. Viewers see three figures standing outside a run-down farmhouse in the pouring rain. One is digging a hole while the two others watch. One of the onlookers sounds distraught, choking out low, guttural moans as thunder cracks in the background. The next scene depicts a bright, sunny baseball field with several young boys playing ball. A player hits the ball beyond a fence, and the boy who had been running after it stops dead in his tracks. He says, "It went on the *Peacock property!*" The ballplayers exchange uncertain glances, and one of them pulls another ball out of his knapsack; the game begins again. The player at bat scuffs his feet, waiting for the pitch. His foot hits something mushy, and when he looks down, he sees blood rising, bubbling up from the dirt. He backs away slowly, staring at the bloodied soil. Ominous music rises with the blood. The other players catch on that something is amiss, and they too back away. The scene cuts to Agent Scully bending over a small rectangular hole in the earth, measuring it and the blade of the shovel that dug it.

Drawing upon an urbanormative trope, Agent Mulder reminisces about his childhood, saying that if he were not "tied to a big city because of his

FBI career," he would settle down and build a home in a place like this. The town or region in this story is not named, but there are several references to the Civil War, including one to "the War of Northern Aggression," and Pittsburgh is mentioned. Thus, the southern-ness of the town is implied. Scully dryly replies, "It'd be like living in Mayberry." At just that moment, the local sheriff arrives, introducing himself as Sheriff Andy Taylor. He thanks the FBI agents for coming, explaining, "It's just me and my deputy, and hell, we've never had anything of this nature." He says the population of home is only a few hundred and "everybody knows everybody." Mulder asks who lives in the run-down farmhouse near the field, saying, "Did you question them? Because they've been watching us the entire time." Sheriff Taylor hesitates, and then says, "That farm belongs to the Peacock family, three boys now, well men. Guess you could call them human. Their folks were in a bad car wreck, and we suppose they died." Scully says, "You *suppose*?" Sheriff Taylor continues, "Well, we tried to administer medical attention, but the boys hauled the bodies away. They haven't been seen for ten years, so we supposed they died."

Scully asks again, "Have you questioned the men?" Three figures can be seen on the porch in the distance. Sheriff Taylor tries to explain, saying, "The Peacocks built that farm during the Civil War. It still has no electricity, no running water, no heat. They grow their own food, they raise their own pigs, they breed their own cows . . . raise and breed their own *stock*, if you get my meaning." Scully insists that as the closest residents to the crime scene, the men must be interviewed, at least as witnesses. Sheriff Taylor says the boys "wouldn't understand." After a long pause, he commences to defend his small town against urban sprawl and the culture of urbanormativity. He says,

> This town is my home. It's quiet, peaceful. I don't even wear a gun. I've seen and heard some of the *sick and horrible things* that go on *outside* my home, and at the same time I knew we couldn't stay hidden forever. One day the modern world would find us and my hometown would change forever. And when I saw *it* in the ground, I knew that day had come. I want to find whoever did this, but in doing so, I'd like it if the way things are around here didn't have to change. I know this is "iffy" Bureau jurisdiction, but I didn't know where else to turn. So, I called the Bureau in Pittsburgh, and when I described the victim, they said I should see you.

Scully and Mulder proceed to the sheriff's office, where they meet Deputy Barney (Pastor, not Fife). They examine the victim in a closet-sized bathroom, because the sheriff wants to keep the investigation out of sight. Scully and Mulder are shown the victim—a horrifically malformed infant, a monstrous birth (Douglas, 1966). Scully, the pathologist of the team, is taken aback by what she sees. She exclaims, "Oh my God, Mulder, it looks as if this child has been afflicted by every rare birth defect known to science. . . . I don't even know where to begin!" Mulder says, "I guess we can rule out murder as the cause of death." Scully says, "I don't know about that." She finds evidence that the child was alive when it was buried. Mulder states, "There's something rotten in Mayberry."

The two agents go outside to discuss the case, trying to determine whether it is an "FBI matter." Scully contends that the child is not the result of a single polygenic mating; "those defects are the result of autosomal dominant disorders, and from the degree . . . mutations that go back many generations." Mulder says, "Sheriff Taylor implied that the boys in the family were not really the type that could easily get dates." Scully recalls the sheriff also implied that they practice inbreeding. She explains, "There are theories which pose that our bodies are simply *vehicles* for genes needing to replicate." Since the agents have been told that there are no females in the Peacock family, they theorize the boys must have kidnapped a woman, because, as Scully puts it, "if the instinct and the need is strong enough, they will answer it anyway that they can." Scully speculates that a woman gave birth to the child, and probably against her will. Since "kidnapping is a Bureau matter," the two forge ahead with their investigation of the Peacocks.

The case only gets more complicated, with layers that fold in upon themselves, like family generations stretching back to the Civil War and beyond. The agents search the Peacock property: their home, their world. The house is empty of the brothers, and the agents find probable cause to enter the premises. Inside, they discover plenty of evidence that there was indeed an unattended birth inside; footprints and a shovel clearly indicate that the infant was the same one buried alive in the field abutting the Peacock land. As Scully and Mulder discuss the need for Sheriff Taylor to arrest the boys, we the viewers can see that they are being watched and heard; a set of eyes surveil the agents. The eyes appear to be hiding beneath the floorboards of the house; they look like part of the house. The agents leave the scene, call Sheriff Taylor, and he agrees that the boys should be arrested in the morning, saying he will obtain the warrants. That night, the Peacock brothers brutally murder both the sheriff and his wife with a club-like instrument.

The next morning, Deputy Pastor is sitting on the sheriff's porch waiting for Scully and Mulder to arrive. He discovered the Taylors' bodies when he came to give the sheriff the DNA test results on the infant. The agents investigate the scene, and Mulder states, "They really went *cavemen* on 'em." Scully's perusal of the DNA reports leads her to determine that the lab must have botched the tests; she comments that there are "far too many gene imbalances, it would have to a lab error, this child's cells would have had to divide triple-fold in cell metaphase." Mulder asks, "Triple. . . . What if each of the Peacock brothers was the father of that child?" Scully replies, "Only one sperm in thousands from a single individual can penetrate an ovum membrane." Mulder says, "What if generations of autosomal breeding could produce such mutations?" Scully says, "There would have to be a weakening of the ovum, and that would have to come from a female member of the Peacock family, and there aren't any left."

Meanwhile, the viewers have learned that the Peacock brothers' mother is alive; it was she beneath the floorboards who overheard Scully and Mulder discussing the arrest of her boys, prompting the attack on the sheriff and his wife. The boys are back at the homestead preparing for the assault on their world by the outsiders. Mrs. Peacock offers moral support. Sounding very much like Sheriff Taylor the day before, she tells her sons:

> They'll be comin' now. We knew this day was gonna happen. That they'd try to change the way things are. All we can do about changin' things is be ready for it—be ready for them. Let them know that this is *our home* and *this is the way it's gonna stay.*

The agents go to the Peacocks with the aid of the deputy, who, within minutes, is killed by a booby-trap set by the brothers. Through the safe distance of their field glasses, Scully and Mulder watch as the brothers move in on the deputy's body "like a pack of animals." He narrates:

> What we're witnessing here is undiluted animal behavior; mankind absent of its own creation of civilization, technology, and information, regressed to an almost prehistoric state, obeying only the often savage laws of nature. We're outsiders invading the den, and trying to take away their one chance of reproducing, which we're gonna do.

Scully and Mulder distract the boys by releasing some pigs from their pen. The agents make their way into the house where they discover Mrs. Peacock under a bed, strapped to a board with wheels. She is dismembered, missing both arms and legs, which, we learn she lost in the car accident that killed her husband. Her other physical deformities, such as her severe facial disfigurements, are presumably the result of inbreeding. She is the missing ovum that Scully and Mulder had speculated they would find, but she is not a kidnapped victim being held against her will. The camera pans to Peacock family photographs adorning the wall. We see generations of Peacocks, all quite similar in appearance, with the telltale facial deformities, but none as monstrous as the brothers. Mrs. Peacock and her husband are posing in one of the photos, and aside from their facial deformities, they look happy, content.

Mrs. Peacock screams at the agents to go away, leave her alone. The agents say they are there to help her; they can get her medical attention. Scully surmises that Edmund, the oldest brother, is both father and brother to the other two. Why she believes this is unclear, since, according to the sheriff, the father has only been dead for ten years, and the other two boys, we learned from Sheriff Taylor before his untimely death, are in their twenties.

Mulder leaves the room to keep an eye on the boys. Scully tries again to talk Mrs. Peacock into leaving the house. She says, *"This is our home—why leave it?!"* Scully says that she must need medical attention. Mrs. Peacock explains how her boys attended to her after the accident using methods the family learned in the "War of Northern Aggression." The mother says, "They're such good boys."

The boys are approaching the house at this point, and Scully runs to help Mulder, leaving Mrs. Peacock behind. There is gunfire and a scuffle; Mulder is in danger. Scully runs back toward Mrs. Peacock, yelling to the boys, "I've got the mother!" One brother was killed in the scuffle, another runs after Scully and is killed by one of the booby traps that he and his brothers had set. In confusion, the other brother disappears. Scully and Mulder look for him and find that he escaped with his mother. They are gone.

Scully and Mulder put out an APB on them, and the police set up a roadblock around a thirty-mile radius. Scully says, "In time we'll catch them." Mulder replies, "I think time already caught them." The show ends with Edmund crawling out of the trunk of the Cadillac. He is talking to his mother, who is also in the trunk.

I dwelled on this episode of the *X-Files* for several reasons. First, it clearly articulates inbred horror; it spells out the mythology in very clear terms. Because of generations of inbreeding, the Peacocks have degenerated into primitive homicidal monsters. The episode illustrates several components of the inbred mythology, stories that define, circumscribe, and distance the supposedly inbred locales from more urbane outsiders (Hayden, 2016, 2014a,b). This particular show is not about any real place. Like many episodes in the *X-Files* series, however, this show reinvents superstitions and beliefs to mine people's fears of what we think *could happen* or *could be true*. The series was known for its ability to tap into age-old folkloric superstitions and fears (Genge, 1995). An episode called "The Jersey Devil" drew upon regional New Jersey lore of the "Leeds Devil," and combined it with "Bigfoot" legends (Genge, 1995, p. 23). In other episodes, the show takes on faith healers, werewolves, ghosts, vampires, cults, witchcraft, demon-possession, cannibalism, and extraterrestrials. As with most superstitions and spooky tales, the proof hardly matters.

THE HORROR WITHIN

The use of inbreeding and the extremely tight-knit, insular community exemplifies the *X-Files'* ability to deploy preexisting fears, speculations, and even partial truths, while updating them for late twentieth to early twenty-first-century television-viewing audiences. The show's propensity to mix folk stories, superstitions, religious beliefs, and science fiction with scientific jargon, as well as the credibility of the U.S. Federal Bureau of Investigation, gives it an air of plausibility. The "Home" episode, in particular, has an aura of facticity established through scientific terminology and references to genetics and DNA testing. The episode also drew upon the dread of extreme insularity and isolation by relying on fears of inbreeding, degeneracy, and the horror within.

The episode reveals many themes of nineteenth-century notions of degeneracy, some of which are made quite explicit and others to which are only alluded. First and foremost, although the show focuses on one inbred family, the story highlights the closeness and insularity of the entire rural town through copious references to "Mayberry," the idyllic, insulated small town of *The Andy Griffith Show* and the sheriff's monologue at the beginning of the show, where he says, "This town is my *home*. It's peaceful, quiet . . . I've seen and heard some of the sick things that go on outside my home, and at the same time I knew we couldn't stay hidden forever. One day the modern world would find us and my hometown would change forever." His sentiments are later mirrored in Mrs. Peacock's warning to her sons as the outsiders are closing in on them. She says, "They'll be comin' now. We knew this day would happen. That they'd try to change the way things are . . . this is our home and this is the way it's gonna stay." Through these two almost identical monologues, the writers situate the theme of inbreeding as the horror within the small, close-knit, tightly integrated community. The sheriff's fears of the modern, outside world polluting his town were unfounded. As in Shirley Jackson's New England towns, the monsters exist within the community, and they are profoundly *un-modern*, regressive, and degenerate. Hence, the Peacocks can be seen as one end on the continuum of the small town's insularity. They are a metonym for the backwardness of the entire town stuck in its Mayberryesque past. This theme is reinforced throughout the show, with references to "everyone knowing everybody" in town and by dwelling on the idea that one need not lock doors in this type of town. Thus, the rest of the town can be seen as only a few steps from the Peacock's, the rottenness seething at the very core of this antiquated town. The Peacocks reside at one extreme end of an insular, inbred spectrum. They are Mayberry run amok.

DEVOLUTIONARY THEORY

Themes of devolution, regression, and degeneracy also run throughout the "Home" episode's narrative. Throughout the show, the three Peacock boys are depicted as atavistic throwbacks on an evolutionary timeline that is steadily marching forward. Agent Mulder says, "They really went 'caveman' on 'em" as he views the bodies of the sheriff and his wife. Later he clarifies his thesis stating, "What we're witnessing here is undiluted, animal behavior—mankind *absent of its own creation of civilization*, technology, and information regressed to an almost prehistoric state, obeying only the often savage laws of nature." And, since the inbrededness of these miscreants has been established through genetic testing, the causality is taken for granted. Inbreeding not only leads to genetic problems and a pronouncement of recessive genetic traits; it *causes* people to devolve into absolute savage primitives. The Peacocks are not fully human; they have returned to a previous state, half-human and half-animal. They are cavemen, emerged from their own cave-like insularity. By shutting out the modern world, keeping civilization at bay, and turning inwards, they have regressed. They are throwbacks to a much earlier time when clubbing people to death and having sex with one's mother were supposedly quite common.

Yet the Peacocks do exist within the modern world. They can drive automobiles and siphon gas; they listen to music and know how to use technologies to their advantage in booby-trapping their house. They have the foresight and are able to put two and two together when they kill the sheriff before he can arrest them. They rig their house when they know the law is bearing down on them. They have human emotions, and like many families, they adorn their walls with pictures of relatives. They are loyal to themselves and their mother. All of these characteristics establish these inbred, rural primitives as close yet far, as savages in the midst of civilization.

As we saw in chapter 2, much of the nineteenth-century literature of degeneration called upon the imagery of the degenerate type existing within the process of modernization and urbanization. Progression forward required "interacting with and creating degenerate spaces near at home" (Stepan, 1985, p. 98). Certain groups have been set aside as necessary and accessible reminders of society's capacity to regress, to devolve. Historian Nancy Stepan noted that "degeneration became a code for other social groups whose behavior seemed sufficiently different from accepted norms as to threaten traditional social relations and the promise of 'progress'" (Stepan, 1985, p. 98). Rural primitives became part and parcel of the rural as wild and rural as deviant themes so central to urbanormativity (Thomas, Lowe, Fulkerson and Smith, 2011; Fulkerson and Thomas, 2014).

The idea that progression necessitates regression was central to many of the nineteenth-century writings on degeneracy, because as Robert Nye observed, the concept of decline is "conceptually inseparable from that of progress" (1985, p. 49). Discussing sociology and degeneracy, he states, "The exponents of a science of society found it impossible to discuss the progressive aspects of social evolution without considering the negative effects that accompanied it, and that threatened to stall or even reverse the 'normal' condition of advance" (1985, p. 49). Similarly, Colin Sumner asserts that the terminology of degeneration and "degenerate type" is still operative today; it has simply been replaced by deviance and "the deviant type" in sociology (1994, p. 136). Fear of social degeneration is still readily apparent as a sign of modernity's tentativeness. Sumner states,

[The growth of the concept of social deviation] was a sign of modernity's self-doubt, a sign of uncertainty about what is normal and about the healthiness of normality. But it was a sign within a utopian discourse which was involved in the cultural reconstruction of the normal, which was a key moment in establishing a stable, corporate society. . . . It was thus a pragmatic holding concept pregnant with its contrary. (Sumner, 1994, p. 136)

The possibility of inbred communities, because they have been constructed as isolated pockets of primitiveness that can crop up in rural locales found throughout the Unites States, offer ready reminders of civilization's contrary tendencies.

STRONG ROOTS

The theme of people tied to place also runs throughout the "Home" episode. It appears as if the land itself germinates these strange, grotesque Peacock creatures. As in Jackson's short stories, part of the Peacock's and the entire town's primitivism is revealed in their immobility and rootedness to ancestral land. The connection to the land is portrayed starkly in one of the first scenes, when the Peacock's blood rises from the soil. Another scene shows Mrs. Peacock's eyes peering from below the floorboards of her ancestral home, as if her dismembered body is embedded in the house itself. This trope of rootedness, embeddedness in the earth and hearth further establishes the Peacocks as regressive and anti-modern. In a modern world where geographical and upward mobility signifies progress and advancement, these territorial people stay below the surface in a chosen state of decline. And, as with the town folk in Jackson's "The Summer People," they turn truly degenerate when their land is intruded upon by outsiders from the modern world. The dialectic of progress and regress, rise and decline, movement forward versus deep-rooted immobility is reinforced in these images of people dug into their dens like animals.

Along with the trope of rootedness to place, the Peacocks are also stuck in time. Throughout the episode, there are numerous references to antiquity, to the family living in the Civil War era without running water, electricity, and other modern amenities. At one point, as the FBI agents plan to approach the Peacock property, the sheriff's deputy instructs them to wear bulletproof vests, because the Peacock brothers have been known to fire Civil War-era muzzleloaders. The deputy yells, "I for one am *not* getting taken out by some antique," which is just what happens. These references to antiques and Civil War weaponry further establish the rural primitives as throwbacks, as unevolved people stuck in both place and time. Similarly, the Peacock brothers are called "the boys" by the sheriff, providing another metaphor for their arrested development and regressiveness. In his discussion of degeneracy and sexuality, Sander Gilman noted that

> the child is the primitive form of man; the primitive is proof of man's earlier attitudes toward sexuality. In this conflation of types of sexual Otherness, the germ of the concept of sexual degeneration is present. Hidden within each individual, capable of being triggered by his fantasy in opposition to his rational mind, is the tendency toward perversion. Perversion is the basic quality ascribed to the sexuality of the Other. Individual perversion is thus seen as proof of the potential perversion of the group. (1985, p. 73)

As both the products of, and participants in, inbreeding, the Peacocks are reminders of society's ability to degenerate, to regress to primitive monsters.

OTHER INBRED HORRORS

To unearth the rural primitive, I have lingered on a few examples of inbred communities in popular culture that clearly illustrate themes of the rural, close-knit community as the degenerate, deviant other to the urbanormative standard. It is important to note, however, that while I have discussed only a few ideal types, the shocking image of inbred, degenerate groups can be found in numerous American horror films. Indeed, the "backwoods horror film" and "hillbilly horror" are now recognized as a genre unto themselves, a genre that traces its heritage to the cult classic, *The Texas Chainsaw Massacre* (dir. Hooper, 1974) featuring a depraved Southern family who kills anyone who ventures into their homestead. When one of the victims escapes to a nearby store, she finds that the owner, who she thought would help her, is also a member of the family and brings her back to the house. The family's primitivism is reinforced as they trot their dead grandparents out of the attic and serve up a dinner of their victims.

The Hills Have Eyes (dir. Craven, 1977), featuring a brutal band of inbred hillbilly cannibals, presents another inbred horror. In the film, we find another group of isolated savages who turn predatory when outsiders intrude upon their territory. This group has the additional gene-altering problem of having been exposed to some type of nuclear testing; however, the fact that they have "taken to the hills" to live away from others in a small group that reproduces itself is also intrinsic to the plot.

Deliverance, both the 1970 James Dickey novel and the 1972 movie (dir. Boorman) based on the book, relies on the notion that isolated, inbred groups are genetically defective and inherently barbaric (see also Thomas et al., 2011; Goad, 1997). The protagonists are outsiders, four men who attempt to escape from the modern, civilized world to the untainted wilderness for a weekend of canoeing and bowhunting. As they meet the locals in a remote region of Georgia, one man mutters, "Talk about genetic deficiencies" as another visitor peers into a shack-like home to see a severely physically disabled girl. Another man plays guitar with a puny looking boy, a banjo aficionado, whose eyes are too small and close together. Aside from his banjo skills, the boy is clearly physically and mentally challenged and does not seem to recognize the men only a few minutes after their encounter. The story does not simply portray these isolated people as having genetic problems and thus pitiable, however. Two of the four weekenders later meet up with two "mountain men" or "toothless bastards" who immediately set out to rape them. One of the locals succeeds in raping one of the outsiders, forcing him to squeal like a pig as he assaults him. They are about to do the same to the other man when the remaining two in the foursome arrive and kill one of the perpetrators. The other flees. The locals in this story are prototypes for degenerate, isolated, backward primitives who have escaped modernity altogether. Throughout the drama, the rural people are depicted as animals, as part of the brutish, unpredictable natural world that the modern, civilized men must battle and overcome (Thomas et al., 2011, pp. 158–161; Goad, 1997, pp. 97–98).

WHITE TRASH TALES, REDNECK
JOKES, AND INBREDEDNESS

As Thomas et al. (2011) and Fulkerson and Thomas (2019, 2016, 2014) illustrate, urbanormativity places rural people and places as the deviant others to the urban norm. This othering of the rural can be relatively harmless, that is, the rural idyll as an escape from city life idea, or it can be utterly horrific as in the horror stories I have discussed. Somewhere in between these two ends of the continuum of rurality are redneck and white trash jokes (cf. Goad, 1997; Roskelly, 1993; Wray and Newitz, 1997). In this brand of humor, rural people are viewed paternalistically as symbolizing the uneducated, backward, and wild, and thus in need of education and taming (Thomas et al., 2011; Fulkerson and Thomas, 2014, 2016, 2019).

Rednecks and white trash are readily available anti-modern primitive types within modernity. As Jim Goad argues, the term "redneck" is "already embossed with stock images . . . the stereotype is so fully fleshed out as to need no explanation" (1997, p. 18). Redneck jokes stand as a constant, humorous reminder that people will tend toward devolution if they are allowed to buck the trend of progress and modernization. The jokes hinge on the assumption that rednecks are stupid, uncivilized, backward, and primitive. Many rely on inbred, incestuous themes, such as you might be a redneck if your family tree has no branches (or looks like a wreath). You might be a redneck is you go to a family reunion to meet Mr. or Mrs. Right, or if your brother-in-law is your uncle. Or, you just might be a redneck if you go Christmas shopping for your mom, your sister, and your girlfriend and you only need to buy one gift. Or, you might be a redneck if your gene pool does not have a deep end, or if you are your own aunt or uncle, or if your dad is your favorite uncle. In the mid-1990s, a list of 283 of these jokes was posted on the internet under the heading "The Canonical List of Redneck Jokes." It concluded with: "Warning: if twenty-five or more of these are true, you should seek *civilized help* immediately!" I was reminded again of the inbreeding leads to degeneracy message recently as I waited at a traffic light behind a pickup truck sporting a bumper sticker that read simply "Discourage Inbreeding." Surrounding the words were smiley-face images, each with something grossly askew, like a hand sticking out of a head, or a mouth on a forehead, or three eyes.

THE FRAILTY OF PROGRESS

Through humor and gothic short stories, cautionary tales and gory movies, there is a lesson to be learned about an insidious devolutionary tendency within our civilization: namely, that progress has not succeeded fully and must be constantly attended to. Modernity contains within it its oppositional figures and contrary tendencies. Because of the mythology of inbrededness—a type of sense-making and an agent of stability based on partial truths and outright lies, incorrect assumptions about genetics, and age-old fears and suspicions—groups of people perceived as inbred and degenerate, such as rural people, rednecks, and bestial mountain men, stand as reminders of this oppositional tendency. Literary critic William Greenslade notes a tendency to fear that which is obscured in the forces of modernization. The belief that larger, progressive changes in society were at the same time spawning dangerous, countervailing forces was crystallized in notions degeneration. He states,

> The belief in the existence of degeneration, or even the suspicion that it existed, fostered a sense that what might really be happening to civilization lay somehow hidden, buried from sight, yet graspable through patient observation of the contours of the surface. . . . Bafflement and disillusionment found release in a theory which seemed to identify the sources of rot. . . . Degeneration provided such a structure. . . . "Degeneration" represented the boundless capacity of a society to "generate" regression: on the one hand, generation and reproduction, on the other decline, degradation, waste. . . . The remarkable grip which the idea secured suggests a permanent secularized "fall" from grace, a structure of feelings of extreme disappointment for which the religious sanctities offered little help. (1994, pp. 15–16)

The late nineteenth-century fields of genetics and heredity captured people's imagination and offered a scientific rhetoric which dovetailed nicely with extant prejudices and fears. For instance, philosopher Sybil Wolfram notes that

> when ordinary people today attribute prohibitions of [consanguineous] unions to the ill effects of inbreeding, specifically that it results in idiot children, this is supposed to be by biological or genetic mechanisms. However, in the past the belief that inbreeding results in idiot children had a different basis which was not biological: "when idiocy did follow consanguineous marriages, as it sometimes would, it was believed to be the fit punishment of some divine law." (1985, p. 145)

Foucault argued that the nineteenth-century middle-class concerns with genealogy "became a preoccupation with heredity" as people scoured their ancestry for possible "defamatory quarters . . . diseases or defects of the group of relatives—the grandfather's general paralysis . . . the hysterical or erotomanic aunts, the cousin with bad morals" (1978, pp. 124–125). In the same period, "the analysis of heredity was placing sex (sexual relations, venereal diseases, matrimonial alliances, perversions) in a position of 'biological responsibility' with regard to the species: not only could sex be affected by its own diseases, it could also . . . transmit diseases or create others that would afflict future generations" (Foucault, 1978, p. 118). Foucault noted how several nineteenth-century "technologies of sex" coalesced in what he called the "perversion-heredity-degenerescence" nucleus. He explained,

Innovations that merged together quite well, for the theory of "degenerescence" made it possible for them to perpetually refer back to one another; it explained how a heredity that was burdened with various maladies (it made little difference whether these were organic, functional, or psychical) ended by producing a sexual pervert . . . but it went on to explain how a sexual perversion resulted in the depletion of one's line of descent—rickets in children, the sterility of future generations. (1978, p. 118)

Similarly, Greenslade notes that, on the whole, "late nineteenth-century positivism did not flinch from the role of moral teacher. In the writings of the major scientific proponents of degeneration, concepts and tropes, which affirm traditional classifications of experience into normal and abnormal, right and wrong, are never far from the surface" (1994, p. 27).

Why are these so-called inbred groups such potent reminders of society's intrinsic tendency toward devolution? Genetic studies have shed more light on recessive gene transmission (or increased homozygosity) within small, isolated populations. Some studies have found that if there is an existing genetic problem within the group, there will be a higher probability that those genes will be transmitted to offspring (see Ottenheimer, 1996; Arens, 1986; Cooley et al., 1990). Not all recessive genes are problematical, and some isolated populations have found non-stigmatizing ways to deal with the increased appearance of these genetic anomalies (Groce, 1985; Wolfram, 1987). Still, other so-called inbred populations have shown no higher incidence of genetic problems than noninbred groups (Ottenheimer, 1996; Wolfram, 1987). Thus, while there is an increased probability for preexisting genetic problems to manifest in inbred groups, there is clearly no evidence that such groups degenerate or devolve to subhuman monsters.

THE INDIVIDUAL BODY VERSUS THE
UNDIFFERENTIATED MASS

What is warded off or suppressed in these types of cautionary tales? As we saw in chapter 2, in *Purity and Danger: An Analysis of the Concepts of Pollution and Taboo* (1966), Mary Douglas asserts that the boundaries of the body symbolize the boundaries of society. She states, "The idea of society is a powerful image. It is potent in its own right to control or to stir men to action. This image has form; it has external boundaries, margins, internal structure. Its outlines contain power to reward conformity and repulse attack. . . . For symbols of society, any human experience of structures, margins or boundaries is ready to hand" (1966, p. 115). The sharing of sexual space in so-called inbred groups and the sharing of bodies in incestuous unions must be prohibited because it threatens the external margins of the self—the corporeal individual. Inbreeding threatens the very notion of the individual body—it represents a blurring of familial lines, but also a blurring of the individual person. This would stand for confusion much more damning than unclear familial roles.

Sex between relatives creates confusion. That confusion would, in turn, cause an internal chaos of the entire system, or, as Sander Gilman stated, "individual perversion is thus seen as proof of the potential perversion of the group" and even the society as a whole (1985, p. 73).

In *The History of Sexuality, Volume One*, Foucault noted that an increased attention paid to controlling individual bodies became a means of controlling the population (1978). As the need to control sexuality increased from the end of the eighteenth century onward, so did the fixation on embodied individuals. As Chris Shilling (1993) also notes, "From the eighteenth century there was a large increase in discourses on sexuality which linked the sex of individual bodies to the management of national problems" (pp. 77–78). This concern with embodied individuals had major consequences in terms of social control. It allowed governments to exert "a far greater degree of control over individuals than had previously been the case" because *"people could be made more separate and different, and hence, more controllable"* (1993, p. 78, emphasis added).

Perhaps the danger of the inbred community is that people are not seen as properly individuated and differentiated, and thus somehow beyond the scope of social control. These groups are over-related; the same blood is running through different bodies, and thus, it is difficult to distinguish one from the other. Discussing the modern, civilized body, Shilling said, "The civilized body characteristic of modern Western societies is highly individualized in that it is strongly demarcated from its social and natural environments" (1993, p. 150). Borrowing from Norbert Elias ([1939] 1978), Shilling notes that there has been a progressive socialization of bodies in modernity and that the "separation of the body from nature helped provide the basis for differentiating between individuals" (1993, pp. 150–151). Elias contended that bodies have become civilized through the processes of socialization, rationalization, and individualization ([1939] 1978, pp. 249–257). Socialization of the body entails hiding natural, biological functions. Rationalization means the body is self-controlled through morals and rational thoughts which "interpose themselves between emotional impulses" (Shilling 1993, p. 166). Rationalization also involves the gradual differentiation of the body; the body itself is broken down into smaller, seemingly separate, parts. Individualization of the body involves people "conceptualizing themselves as separate from others, with the body acting as a container for the self" (Shilling, 1993, p. 166). Elias noted that individualization of private, separate bodies is "now so self-evident that it is rarely questioned," yet the nature of this boundary is "never properly explained" ([1939] 1978, p. 249). He argued that the notion of individuated bodies caused people to construct an "affective wall between their bodies and those of others," wherein people are conceived as "hermetically closed individuals" ([1939] 1978, pp. 249–250). In modern societies, the civilized body is marked by its distance from nature and its distance from other bodies, and the flesh of humans became a source of embarrassment as extreme measures of privacy were enacted. This is not a pre-social state, but it has been socially created through what Elias calls civilizing processes ([1939] 1978, p. 250).

In the mythology of inbrededness, several powerful, and powerfully modern, notions are called upon to assemble the rural, insular, isolated community as inherently degenerate, primitive, and horrific. First and foremost are the misconceptions and partial understandings about heredity and genetic transmission in isolated groups, which are entwined and shored up with age-old notions of inbreeding leading to monstrosities in offspring. The belief that the children of inbreeding would inevitably be of a lesser stock and somehow physically and/or mentally malformed became unquestioned common knowledge.

Second, in the idea of the inbred community, sexuality is brought to the fore. These communities are circumscribed by a form of degenerate sexuality. Inbreeding connotes loveless sex and procreation among too closely related people. They are said to breed like animals in the barnyard. It suggests a sharing of sexual space where sex is a common event; they do it all the time. The hegemonic view of truly proper sexual relations is that which occurs between two heterosexual, consenting, unrelated, monogamous, romantically involved adults. Thus the sexual horde of indistinguishable family members is a particularly damning image.

Third, the notion of inbreeding connotes a group of people known only as a collectivity. They are tribal, clannish, closed off to others. Their bodies are not fully individuated; their minds are not properly civilized. If you intrude upon them, they will descend upon you en masse. Like late nineteenth-century notions of crowds, which were also described in terms "heavily indebted to organicist socio-biology rhetoric" (Greenslade, 1994, p. 23), any form of collectivity was highly suspected, as regressive and primitive in evolutionary terms. Instead of fully individuated persons, collectivities "tended toward homogeneity" (Greenslade, 1994, p. 23, see also Pick, 1989). Similarly, Raymond Williams discusses romantic notions of our rural past signifying "wholeness," but a wholeness that is inherently primitive and childlike when viewed in evolutionary terms, from the perch of urbanormativity and its heterogeneous, modern, cosmopolitan worldview (Williams, 1973; see also Clifford, 1986; Thomas, Lowe, Fulkerson and Smith, 2011; Fulkerson and Thomas, 2019, 2014). Homogeneity is assumed in inbred communities. Because they're all related, one person is indistinguishable from the next. They are a collectivity that chooses to not mix with others, preferring their own company and abhorring strangers, to the point of attacking them. This is clearly a problem in a modern, individuated, rational, and contractually based society.

The mythology of inbrededness tapped into the larger mythology of degeneration, which installed an alternative myth to that of progress. This alternative myth spoke to the dark side of progress (Greenslade, 1994; Chamberlin and Gilman, 1985). Inbreeding is seen as particularly insidious as it is a corruption by blood—an irreversible decline. It presents a secular, modern, and genetic fall from grace constructed to replace previously intact religious falls from grace—the antithesis of the cosmopolitan, urbane norm. In chapter 4, I follow the mythology of inbrededness and stories of the rural primitive into the twenty-first century where it has been recycled and made anew in more recent horror films. As I discuss, much of the mythology remains the same, but has only become more skewed and detached from rural realities.

NOTE

1. An earlier version of this chapter appeared in G. M. Fulkerson and Thomas, A. R. (2014). *Studies in Urbanormativity*. Lanham, MD: Lexington Books. Reprinted by permission.

Chapter 4

Inbred Horror Revisited[1]

The Rural Primitive in Twenty-First-Century Backwoods Horror Films

As I discussed in previous chapters, inbred horror is the fear of the rural people and places as monstrous, insular, and dangerous due to isolation and presumed inbreeding, or sexual relations and procreation among closely related people (Hayden, 2014a,b). In chapter 3, I looked at popular cultural examples of depictions of rural, close-knit communities as the degenerate, deviant other to an urban, normative standard (cf. Hayden, 2014a, p. 181; Fulkerson and Thomas, 2019; Fulkerson and Thomas, 2016; Fulkerson and Thomas, 2014; Cloke and Little, 1997). I considered the messages that these inbred horror stories relay to their audiences: small, rural, tight-knit communities in which "everyone is related" and "everyone knows everyone" have come to signify, for those on the outside, a cautionary tale. Rural communities are constructed as backward; they are degenerate, anti-modern, and anti-urban (cf. Fulkerson and Thomas, 2019; Fulkerson and Thomas, 2016; Fulkerson and Thomas, 2014). In the urban-rural divide and cultural ideal of urbanormativity (cf. Fulkerson and Thomas, 2019; Fulkerson and Thomas, 2014; Thomas, Lowe, Fulkerson and Smith, 2011), the message of the tight-knit community is clear: primitivism, savagery, regression, degeneracy, and an overall devolution will result if groups are allowed to become too close, too insular, too familiar (Hayden, 2014a,b, 2016; Hayden; Fulkerson and Thomas, 2014, 2019).

In this chapter, I extend my analysis of these widely held misrepresentations of rural life and show how they allow urban or suburban dwellers to distance themselves from these supposedly inbred and grotesque rural others. By closely examining and interrogating this rural cultural bogeyman—and they are almost always men—my goal is to provide a more nuanced understanding of how social representations of the rural have become increasingly skewed and distant from reality while reinforcing urban life as the normal

Figure 4.1   Screenshot from the *Wrong Turn* movie. *Source*: Photograph taken by author.

state of affairs (Fulkerson and Thomas, 2019; Fulkerson, 2016). I also consider structural and spatial issues of inequality that both cause and result from rural misrepresentations (Fulkerson and Thomas, 2019). How does this particular form of rural othering operate to reproduce inequalities and allow for the real social ills that affect people in rural areas to go unnoticed? No direct line can be drawn from stereotypes of rural people as inbred, degenerate monsters to, for instance, the relative lack of media coverage of the 2010 West Virginia coal mine explosion that killed twenty-nine miners. Because the stereotypes and caricatures of rural people as monstrous others have become hegemonic, however, these images play into what DeKeseredy, Muzzati, and Donnermeyer call a "masking or 'conscious disguise' of real issues about crime, violence, and gender relations in rural contexts" (2014, p. 19). If popular culture imagery constantly reminds us that rural folks are scary monsters, why should we care if they die in explosions deep in the mines of West Virginia?

In this chapter, I continue to explore inbred horror themes, focusing specifically on the film genre known as backwoods horror movies. The stock image of scary, inbred rural folk has become such an identifiable characterization in movies that backwoods horror films, also known as "hillbilly horror/slasher," "cabin horror" (Grant, 2014), and even "inbred movies," are now recognized as genres unto themselves. For example, a film critic's list of "The Top 25 Backwoods Horror & Suspense Movies" was compiled by Mark H. Harris for About.com and the Bloody Disgusting website published its "The Top 10 Inbred Movies of All Time" (Hayden, 2014, 2016; DeKeseredy, Muzzatti, and Donnermeyer, 2014; Murphy, 2013). In an article about the horrification and pornification of rural culture, DeKeseredy et al. state that "in-depth content analysis of rural horror movies and pornographic media are required to provide better answers to questions" about gender, race, and violence (among other issues) and "many critical criminologists are well-suited to take on these tasks" (2014, p. 192). In this chapter, I conduct a content analysis of a purposive sample from the backwoods horror movie genre, looking closely at one archetypal inbred horror film franchise: the *Wrong Turn* movies, of which there are six.

WHY THE *WRONG TURN* MOVIES?

The *Wrong Turn* movies may seem, at first glance, to be unworthy of any serious academic consideration. These are not good cinematic works by any measure. Perhaps metaphorically, the final two films in the series devolve to the point of being unwatchable. There are several reasons to pay close attention to these films if we are to understand the making and remaking of the inbred, rural primitive horror mythology in the twenty-first century.

This collection of films was selected for a detailed analysis for three reasons: (1) the movies traffic in the types of exaggerated, grotesque, monstrous rural imagery that I am studying It's really all they have to offer the viewers, and the films just keep churning up these images and making them more and more horrific as the franchise goes on. (2) The time span in which the films emerged and the longevity of the franchise is important. And (3) the movies have been profitable; people are watching them.

First and foremost, the theme of rural, isolated people inbreeding and degenerating into subhuman, cannibalistic monsters runs throughout the collection of films and grows more and more grotesque and outlandish over the course of the franchise. While the filmmakers try to add some new twist or element to each installment, the basic conceit remains throughout: a small group (usually about six to eight) of young, attractive, middle-class, mostly white adult detours and gets lost in the Appalachian hills of West Virginia. While they try to make their way through the woods, they are attacked by three grossly malformed men whose ages are hard to estimate, given their horrific countenances. The viewers come to know these three brothers as the Hillickers: Three Fingers, One Eye, and Sawtooth. The brothers appear, in one form or another, in each of the films. That they are the result of inbreeding is established as the opening credits roll in the original *Wrong Turn* film. Printed pages with the words "genetic mutations" and "facial deformities due to inbreeding" flash on the screen. In later films, the inbrededness of the people is hinted at through references to "inbred hillbillies," "hillbilly freaks," and "banjo-playing rednecks." These terms are already embossed with meaning and are enough to signify the inbred monsters to come.

Second is the time span in which the films emerged: 2003 through 2014. There has been scarce academic attention paid to backwoods horror films, but much of the small body of literature that exists tends to focus on rural-themed horror films of the 1960s and 1970s, most notable are *Two Thousand Maniacs!* (1964), *Deliverance* (1972), better characterized as a backwoods suspense/thriller film, *The Texas Chainsaw Massacre* (1974), and *The Hills Have Eyes* (1977)—progenitors of all subsequent backwoods horror films (cf. Clover, 1992; Bell, 1997; Sharrett, 1984; Rodowick, 1984). There are some excellent newer additions to the literature on backwoods horror films, but these works do not focus specifically on the long-running *Wrong Turn* film franchise (see DeKeseredy, Muzzatti, and Donnermeyer, 2014; Murphy, 2013). I focus on the *Wrong Turn* films because they bring the inbred horror mythology into the new century and inculcate it, over and over again, to legions of (mostly) young viewers.

The original *Wrong Turn* movie was released in theaters in 2003 by Summit Entertainment. After the original, all of the subsequent films were released by Twentieth Century Fox Home Entertainment and went straight-to-DVD or on-demand formats. The sequel, *Wrong Turn 2: Dead End*, came out in 2007, and then a *Wrong Turn* film was released almost every two years, give or take, until the last installment, *Wrong Turn 6: Last Resort*, in 2014 (see table 4.1). There is some talk in online forums of a *Wrong Turn* 7 coming sometime in 2020, but these rumors are unconfirmed (see *MGDSQUAN*, May 7, 2015, on http://www.horrorsociety.com and Todd Rigney May 30, 2015, on http://www.dreadcentral.com).

Since the *Wrong Turn* movies emerged around the turn of the millennium and continued well into the first decade and a half of the new millennium, we can look closely at how and why the themes of inbred horror are reconstructed and recreated in current American popular culture. Why do these images still tap into the imagination of the horror-viewing public? The *Wrong Turn* movies rely heavily on the inbred rural tropes established in earlier rural horror films, especially *The Texas Chainsaw Massacre*, and exploit them over and over again for all they are worth. They recycle centuries-old misconceptions

Table 4.1   *Wrong Turn* Films and Year Released

Film	Year Released
Wrong Turn	2003
Wrong Turn 2: Dead End	2007
Wrong Turn 3: Left for Dead	2009
Wrong Turn 4: Bloody Beginnings	2011
Wrong Turn 5: Bloodlines	2012
Wrong Turn 6: Last Resort	2014

about inbreeding in rural areas and shore up damaging notions about rural people. Some of the messages have stayed true to the original backwoods horror films of the 1970s; some have been expanded and broadcast new messages to new audiences.

Finally, I focus on these movies because they have been, at least until the final installment, profitable. While details on the exact amount of money earned by the films are hard to ascertain, since there are six of them, they must have brought in some returns or Twentieth Century Fox would have put an end to them.

According to three movie data websites—TMDb: The Movie Database (https://www.themoviedb.org/), IMDb: The Internet Movie Database (http://www.imdb.com/), and The Numbers: Where Data and the Movie Business Meet (http://www.the-numbers.com/)—the *Wrong Turn* franchise did indeed turn a profit. The data are incomplete since only the first film made it to the box office. Further, there are no data available on *Wrong Turn 5: Bloodlines.* It is difficult to ascertain profits from streaming and other straight-to-DVD or on-demand forums. But after totaling up the available earnings minus the production budgets, I estimated the net earnings for all six films to be anywhere from around $25,000,000 to $32,000,000 (see table 4.2). I also was not able to find any data on marketing and other expenses, so this is a rough estimate (see also *MGDSQUAN*, May 7, 2015, on http://www.horrorsociety.com/).

While the law of diminishing returns clearly operates for the *Wrong Turn* franchise, overall, the films sold, and the horror-viewing public bought their messages of rural people as inbred, degenerate, grotesque, violent, cannibalistic, insular monsters who will attack any interlopers who dare enter their home. These themes have been profitable enough that the online discussions of a seventh installment seem plausible (see https://www.facebook.com/WrongTurn7Movie/ and *MGDSQUAN*, May 7, 2015, on http://www.horrorsociety.com/).

Horror films, even bad ones, are allegories. What lessons are learned from these films, and are they the same lessons conveyed over and over again?

Table 4.2   Estimated Profits for *Wrong Turn* Franchise

Film	Year and Format	Estimated Production Costs ($)	Estimated Sales ($)	Estimated Profits ($)
Wrong Turn	2003, Theater	10,000,000	28,649,556	18,649,556
WT2: Dead End	2007, DVD	4,000,000	9,009,641	5,009,651
WT3: Left for Dead	2009, DVD	2,000,000	5,689,328	3,689,328
WT4: Bloody Beginnings	2011, DVD	2,000,000	3,148,521	1,148,521
WT5: Bloodlines	2012, DVD	No Data	No Data	No Data
WT6: Last Resort	2014, DVD	1,200,000	1,008,317	−191,683
Total (approximate)		15,600,000	47,505,363	31,905,363

Do these films offer any new cautionary tales? What is warded off in these monster stories?

INCEST AND INBRED IMAGERY

The fact that the Hillickers are the products of, and ostensibly engage in, inbreeding is established early in the first *Wrong Turn*. The opening scene flashes the words that clearly convey the message in black-and-white print. The opening also presents the severe physical deformities of the three brothers—appearances so grotesque that there is no question that they are inbred and inbreeding has caused them to devolve, to degenerate, and to become less than human. It is closeness to a fault. They share genetic material like hand-me-downs; their chromosomes have become frayed and defective.

The three brothers are animal-like, making only grunting and snorting noises that they seem to understand. While these are heightened, exaggerated stereotypes of inbred rural folk, they are not new. These images were the stock-in-trade of earlier backwoods horror films such as *The Texas Chainsaw Massacre* and *The Hills Have Eyes*. A new twist on the inbreeding leading to degeneracy theme emerges when the viewers learn that the Hillickers' inbrededness also seems to allow them to *regenerate*. Especially in films two through six, the Hillicker brothers are indestructible.

The theme of the monster that cannot be killed runs throughout horror movies and especially horror film franchises. But in this collection, the filmmakers attribute their *inability* to feel pain and their *ability* to regenerate to congenital abnormalities due to inbreeding. This idea is made obvious in the prequel segment of *Wrong Turn 4: Bloody Beginnings* when the young Hillicker boys are behind bars in the "Glenville Sanatorium" in West Virginia. A doctor describes the boys as having a congenital disease that results in their inability to feel physical pain; he also says they are "extremely smart and dangerous." This asylum scene is borrowed from another horror franchise, the *Halloween* films, and thus not new to the horror genre. What is new, though, is that the inbred, rural, hillbilly monsters are described as extremely smart and as possessing almost superhuman abilities—they can withstand physical pain. This assertion that they are smart, or cunning, is reinforced when the boys use a bobby pin to break out of their cell and release all the other patients in the sanatorium. The boys proceed to cannibalize the nearest orderly.

CANNIBALISM

Cannibalism in rural horror films is also nothing new—it was firmly established in the 1960s with *Two Thousand Maniacs!* and then reified in the films of the 1970s. The *Wrong Turn* movies are nothing if not derivative of these earlier films. Cannibalism runs throughout the *Wrong Turn* movies and grows more gruesome and outlandish with installment. For instance, by the *Wrong Turn 6: Last Resort*, the outsiders are being skinned and eaten alive; people's brains are consumed while their blood is still pumping; and the Hillicker brothers drink the blood of live victims as they hang upside down from trees. As with earlier rural horror movies, the root cause or reason for the cannibalism is never revealed—it's simply part and parcel to their degeneracy. Perhaps once you have broken the incest taboo, all taboos are fair game, so why not eat people?

In two of the *Wrong Turn* sequels, the reason for the Hillickers' cannibalism is suggested, however. In *Wrong Turn 2: Dead End* and *Wrong Turn 5: Bloodlines*, we learn that there has also been an environmental spill or disaster of some sort related to the paper mill that used to operate in the region. The chemicals from the old mill have killed off all of the wildlife in the region, so naturally, they must eat any strangers who wander into the vicinity. In homage to *The Hills Have Eyes*, the chemicals also appear to have had a hand in the genetic abnormalities suffered by the inbred locals, as two victims in *Wrong Turn 2: Dead End* stumble upon the abandoned paper mill and find large barrels of chemicals labeled "Causes Birth Defects." This environmental storyline is dropped by the final installment, *Wrong Turn 6: Last Resort*, which features a deer hunting scene, so the wildlife seems to have returned to the area. In the end, the Hillickers are back to eating people because that is what inbred monsters do.

ROOTEDNESS IN PLACE AND TIME

A central theme in the mythology of inbreeding is rootedness to the region, to the very soil from which these horrific creatures spring (Hayden, 2014a, 2016). This theme is illustrated in the *Wrong Turn* films through camera angles and cinematography making the brothers appear as part of the woods themselves. They peer, unseen by their prey, from behind trees; they move undetected through the wilderness; they are part of the land. They have animal-like senses of smell and hearing. They are territorial and protect their home through elaborate and barbaric booby traps, always involving barbed wire, which the films establish as a rustic, backwoods signifier.

The notion of a people that time forgot, like the theme of rootedness to ancestral home, also constructs the Hillickers as rooted, mired, bogged down. It is an anti-modern, anti-urban image. In a postmodern world where geographical and upward mobility is the norm, movement stands for progress and advancement, but these territorial people stay tied to the land in a chosen state of decline. And they turn truly degenerate when their land is intruded upon by outsiders from the modern world who often barge right into their cabin in the woods (Murphy, 2013). As Matthew Grant, a film studies scholar, notes of cabin horror, "The cabin and the surrounding wilderness gain a malevolent agency through their almost sentient role as an obstacle and isolating influence. . . . An isolated cabin, removed from society and any meddling institutions" (2014, pp. 5–6). Grant draws on the earlier work of film critic Robin Wood who argued that horror films represent the return of the repressed or put quite simply, "Normality is threatened by the monster" (Wood, quoted in Greven, 2019, p. 3). The films expose the tension between progress and regress, rise and decline, movement forward versus deep-rooted immobility and reinforce in earlier popular culture images of people hunkered into their rustic cabin (Hayden, 2014a). Urbanormativity struggles against the idea of rurality, an idea that is appealing to those who resist the constant push for change, progress, movement.

In some of the later films in the *Wrong Turn* series, this theme of rootedness in place and time is betrayed when the locations of the films change. While all the films take place in West Virginia, in some installments the Hillicker brothers leave their den and the woods. It is hard to know if this change is a statement about newfound mobility among this inbred group or if it is the result of sloppy screenwriting and writers running out of story lines in the woods.

In *Wrong Turn 4: Bloody Beginnings* the setting changes. We learn that as youngsters in 1974, the three brothers were rounded up and put in a sanatorium because they were found standing over the dead bodies of their parents. No further explanation is given on this matter. When the film flashes forward to 2003, we find that the three brothers, now adults, live in the since-abandoned sanatorium, even though in earlier films they resided deep in the West Virginia woods.

In *Wrong Turn 5: Bloodlines*, the rootedness motif is dropped again. In this film, the Hillickers are on the move in a town called Fairlake, West Virginia, to free a relative (father or grandfather, this is not fully explained) from jail. The population of Fairlake, the viewers learn, completely disappeared in 1817. The locals and college kids that flock to the town once a year for a music festival, the "Mountain Man Festival," believe the 1817 townsfolk were eaten by mountain cannibals. This film has more inconsistencies than I can count, but in an interesting turn of events, the brothers are not only mobile, but they also figure out how to disable the entire town's cell towers and power sources, thus enabling them to free their captive relative and slaughter many concertgoers. The film series is fraught with temporal and storyline inconsistencies, so it is likely that these two departures from the rootedness theme are not significant, but the brothers' ability to disable an entire region's power sources marks a major leap ahead for people who have been portrayed as atavistic throwbacks to an earlier time and place.

Gender among the Inbred

The unfortunate fates of female victims in slasher films have been considered in the academic literature on horror films (see Clover, 1992; DeKeseredy et al., 2014; Murphy, 2013). Most female characters do not fare well in the horror genre as a whole, although typically one young woman still lives to tell the tales at the end of many of horror films. The original *Wrong Turn* film and several subsequent installments hold true to this "last girl standing" formula. Girls or women as inbred monsters in horror films, however, have received little to no academic attention. This is most likely because inbred monsters in backwoods horror films are almost solely represented by men—brothers. In all but two of the *Wrong Turn* films, inbred girls or women are absent. Inbreeding seems to result in predominantly male offspring who possess hypermasculine strength and brutality. However, in *Wrong Turn 2: Dead End*, some grossly malformed female characters appear. In one scene, a young adult woman is shown giving birth in a filthy cabin in the woods. She squats briefly and a monster child is born. The same female appears in a later scene wherein she and her mate are having sex in the woods—they rut like animals. This same character is also shown perpetrating some violence, but her role centers mainly around sex and breeding. Also, in *Wrong Turn 2*, an older couple, male and female, seem to represent the matriarch and patriarch of the inbred family, but the female elder does not take part in a lot of the action in the film.

Wrong Turn 6: Last Resort features a key female figure. In this film, an urban outsider learns that he has inherited an inn, the Hot Springs Hotel, in the remote woods of West Virginia. He and a small group of his friends set off from New York to find the place, and when they come upon the inn, a young man and woman, a couple, are working at the reception desk. The two are not "inbred looking." They suffer from no noticeable facial abnormalities. Yet the male calls the female "sister" as they kiss romantically. As the film develops, or devolves, we learn that the "normal looking" brother and sister are related to the Hillickers who work at the inn, butchering and serving human flesh to unsuspecting guests. Here again, we find the Hillickers are uprooted from the cabin in the woods.

We also learn that the sister, Sally, is unable to conceive with any available family members due to years of inbreeding. She needs Danny, the newcomer, the outsider who inherited the inn. Danny is a family member, but not so closely related. She hopes that mating with him will produce a child. Sally is portrayed as hypersexual—she even uses an almost dead male victim as a sex toy. She is driven by her desire to breed. As she pursues Danny, she tells him, "Your blood, our blood beats inside us." Later, Danny is brought to meet his "extended family" deep in the woods beyond the inn. Sally tells Danny that these are all his kin, explaining that there are three original families in the woods: the Creightons, the Bogles, and the Hillickers. Danny is surrounded by inbred monsters, males and females, each more deformed than the last. Sally asks Danny, "How do we preserve our family strength? We keep to our own." She goes on to explain that the genetic abnormalities are the "price of purity." That night, Danny has sex with Sally. In the final scene of the film, Danny is the lone survivor from the group of outsiders with whom he arrived. He has chosen his kin over his friends, all of whom have died gruesome deaths at the hands of Three Fingers, One Eye, and Sawtooth. Danny stays at the hotel with Sally, presumably to carry on the inbred family lineage.

In this final scene of the final *Wrong Turn* movie (to date), we see a woman introduced as a key inbred protagonist. She is over-sexed, forceful in her singular pursuit of procreation, and her mission is tightly bound to the inbreeding and degeneracy themes that run through all the films. She is presented as a female rural stereotype—a hyper-sexualized breeder, but she is given some agency as she acts to procure a suitable related partner with whom to continue the inbred bloodline.

In the *Wrong Turn* franchise, as in earlier inbred horror stories, several powerful, and powerfully modern, notions are called upon to assemble the rural, insular, isolated community as inherently degenerate, primitive, and horrific (Hayden, 2014a). Misconceptions and partial understandings about heredity and genetic transmission in isolated groups are entwined and shored up with age-old notions of inbreeding, leading to genetically malformed offspring. The belief that the children of inbreeding would inevitably be monstrous and somehow physically and/or mentally malformed has been challenged scientifically, yet it became unquestioned common knowledge in nineteenth-century America (Hayden, 2014a). In the *Wrong Turn* film franchise, this conventional wisdom is reborn, recycled, and reinvigorated in the new millennium with inbred horror tales that work to teach this notion to a new generation of horror fans, thus guaranteeing that these stereotypes will continue to permeate the popular culture and imagination for years to come.

In the imagery of the inbred community, sexuality is front and center. Inbred, rural people are circumscribed by the perception that they practice a form of degenerate sexuality. Inbreeding connotes loveless sex and procreation among too closely related people (Hayden, 2014a). They are said to breed like animals in the barnyard or to rut like wildlife in the forest, as in *Wrong Turn 2: Dead End*. As Robin Wood, a leading scholar of the horror genre, put it, "Otherness represents that which the bourgeois ideology cannot recognize or accept but must be dealt with (as Barthes suggests in *Mythologies*) in one of two ways: either by rejecting it and if possible annihilating it, or by rendering it safe and assimilating it, converting it as far as possible into a replica of itself" (1979, p. 27). Rob Shields in *Places on the Margin: Alternative Geographies of Modernity* makes a similar point:

> In this way, "margins" become signifiers of everything "centres" deny or repress; margins as "the Other" become the condition of possibility of all social and cultural entities. In these "centres," self-centered and entrenched groups inflate their opinions to ostensibly universal proportions, glossing over differences between centre and periphery, with the help of thought constraints and banishment to exile if necessary. (1991, p. 296)

The rural primitive other stands in such stark contrast to the urbanormative center that it must be repressed. The *Wrong Turn* movies represent the continued attempt to reject and repress that which cannot be annihilated—the inbred monsters will not die.

Another damning perception of supposedly inbred people is that they are tribal, clannish, closed off to others. Their bodies are not fully individuated; their minds not properly civilized (Hayden, 2014a). They are too familiar, sharing flesh and blood among the group, like communal property. And, as we see so graphically illustrated throughout the *Wrong Turn* films, if you intrude upon them, they will descend upon you en masse. They are a collectivity that chooses to not mix with others. This is clearly a problem in a postmodern, individuated, geographically mobile, and technological society. The result of this extreme urbanormativity is that rural people are simply and profoundly *not like us*. The mythology of inbredness taps into the larger mythology of degeneration—it glimpses the dark underbelly of progress (Hayden, 2014a). Inbreeding is a corruption by blood, an irreversible decline. And it is the opposite of a cosmopolitan, urbane norm. At the turn of the new millennium, the *Wrong Turn* films remind us again and again of the frailty of progress. We must continue to push forward, or we tempt a fate like that of the Hillickers: degenerate, malformed, and grossly disfigured.

URBAN CENTER AND RURAL MARGINS

In Kathleen Stewart's ethnography of abandoned West Virginia coal camps, the author explores the idea of a space that resists capitalism, modernism, and urbanormative standards. She acknowledges that these pockets can be found across the American cultural landscape, from backwoods New England to rural California. As she puts it,

> In the two political imaginaries of center and margin there is a telltale contrast: the one, relatively self-assured and oblivious to its privilege, delimits clean lines

of will and action to leave its mark on the world, while the "Other" raids and poaches, stays at the ready to take advantage of opportunities that come along . . . and sifts through signs of its own otherness . . . for something of lasting value. The one might come to imagine itself as structure and order while the "Other," with no power to keep the surrounding other at a distance sees itself in moments of engagement and encounter and the sheer nervous movement of contingency and indeterminacy. (Stewart, 1996, p. 42)

Inbred horror movies in popular culture reify the rural primitive other and maintain rural people's distance from the urbanormative center. Robin Wood, writing about the horror film, stated, "One might say that the true subject of the horror genre is the struggle for all that our civilization represses or oppresses" (1979, p. 28). But as the regenerating monsters in *Wrong Turn* teach us, unsolved problems return; they refuse to be repressed.

The theme of the 2015 Rural Sociological Society's Annual Meetings in Madison Wisconsin was "Knowing Rural." Conference attendees were reminded that

> making sense of rural experiences requires understanding the diverse geographies, economies, and communities that make up rural places. After all, rural landscapes include sites of high-amenity recreation, industrialized agriculture production, chemical processing plants, prisons and pocket-size organic farms. And these sites are undergoing significant change. As rural population's age and rural communities confront the emergent complexities of contemporary life, the lived experience of rurality is undergoing rapid transformation. (RSS 2015 Conference Program)

Stereotypes of rural people perpetuated in popular culture as inbred, monstrous, homicidal, and cannibalistic maniacs hinder this type of knowledge of the real, lived lives of rural people. This form of othering allows outsiders to disregard rural people and to view them as not fully human. Their exploitation by the coal industry, paper mills, fracking for natural gas, or the fishing or logging industries is not an issue; their lack of health care is not a concern. They only appear in the media as curiosities or monstrosities, so why should we be concerned about their intergenerational poverty? They bring problems like methamphetamine addiction upon themselves, don't they?

In Donnermeyer and DeKeseredy's book *Rural Criminology* (2014), the authors call for a critical criminological perspective within studies of rural crime. If we continue to see rural people as homicidal maniacs, we will not recognize the real, lived experiences of the diverse residents of rural places, including both victims and perpetrators of real rural crimes—domestic violence, arson, burglaries of farm equipment, drug dependency, such as the abuse of oxycodone which started as a rural drug problem—a campaign by big pharma to distribute as many possible addictive opioids in rural areas—and spread into cities and suburbs and is now linked to the heroin abuse plaguing the United States.

CAN WE TALK ABOUT RURALITY IN POPULAR CULTURE WITHOUT TALKING ABOUT MONSTERS?

There are a few newer movies that critique or even parody the stereotypes of the backwoods horror film genre. *Tucker and Dale vs. Evil* (2012) offers a great example of a film that turns these "backwoods folks as inbred monsters" tropes on their heads. Set in the Appalachian Mountains in West Virginia, the film follows two harmless, kind-hearted rural young men—locals—who buy an old shack in the middle of the woods to fix up as a retreat for fishing. The men, Tucker and Dale, are happened upon by a group of college students who tell scary stories of college students who, while on a Memorial Day outing twenty years earlier, are murdered by the locals. In the *Dale and Tucker* plot, though, the college students are so hapless that they seem to be throwing themselves into harm's way while in the vicinity of Dale and Tucker. The two locals try to help these accident-prone youths; for example, they come to the aid of a young female co-ed, Allison, who fell into the water near their fishing boat. They bring her to their cabin so she can recuperate. Her friends, of course, think the protagonists have brought her there to eat her, just like the locals do in all of the backwoods horror films. As the story unfolds, more and more of the college students get killed off by their own haplessness and reliance on stereotypes. For instance, one college guy runs into a tree, impaling himself with a branch because he sees Tucker waving around a chainsaw. What the victim does *not* see is that Tucker just ran into a bees' nest with his chainsaw and is waving it around, looking very much like Leatherface from *The Texas Chainsaw Massacre*, in an attempt to get the bees away from him. The entire movie follows this narrative of Tucker and Dale trying to help the helpless city-folk, but still appearing as though they are out to get them.

A similar parody is presented in the *Harold and Kumar Go to White Castle* sequel, titled *Harold and Kumar Escape from Guantanamo Bay* (2008). The film features a sequence in which the protagonists stumble upon a backwoods scene that inverts many hillbilly horror stereotypes. The backwoods people are helpful and hospitable; their trailer is neat as a pin; the man of the house is a fastidious clean freak. The inbred stereotype rears its ugly head, however, when Harold and Kumar stumble upon the couple's cycloptic son, who was hidden in the basement. The basement of a trailer you ask? It's a stoner movie. Here the inbred boy, the cyclops, serves to illustrate how ridiculous the inbred monster stereotypes are, which is certainly a step forward in the popular imagery of rurality. These satires also further illustrate just how taken-for-granted the rural stereotypes in horror films have become.

A more serious example of rural people in cinema being depicted in a much more nuanced way is *Winter's Bone* (2010). The film is not a horror film, although it does include one scene that could be perceived as gory. *Winter's Bone* is a drama and suspense film set in a rural place. This critically acclaimed film, based on the 2006 Daniel Woodrell novel of the same title, focuses on Ree, played by Jennifer Lawrence. Ree is a teenaged girl trying to keep her family together in the face of extreme poverty in the very rural Ozarks. The movie paints an unromantic, realistic portrait of a strong female protagonist who is not the victim or perpetrator of a bloody crime; she does not wear cut-off jean shorts. She and her family survive through her strength and grit. Jennifer Lawrence starred in *Winter's Bone* before she was cast as Catniss Everdeen in *The Hunger Games* series, and there are some interesting parallels to be drawn between these two strong female characters from rural settings.

Scholars of rural people and places must continue to ask, "Can we talk about rural people, places, and culture without talking about inbred monsters?" In chapter 5, I examine rural true crime television for depictions of rurality within this fast-growing television genre. In these true crime retellings, TV producers may not be telling monster tales, but they are relying on the rural-as-scary aesthetic found in inbred horror films such as the *Wrong Turn* franchise. And in chapter 6, I look to new rural imagery of the late twentieth to early twenty-first centuries such as those presented in *Tucker and Dale vs. Evil* and *Winter's Bone*. I discuss these examples in greater length as well as other areas within popular culture that present more nuanced examples of rural imagery, working against the stereotypes of rural people and places as scary, violence-prone, and dangerous.

NOTE

1. An earlier version of this chapter appeared in G. M. Fulkerson and Thomas, A. R. (2016). *Reimagining rural: Urbanormative portrayals of rural life*. Lanham, MD: Lexington Books.

Chapter 5

Murder Comes to Town[1]

The Rural Primitive on True Crime Television

In chapter 4 I examined rural-themed horror films, known as "hillbilly horror," or "backwoods horror," "inbred horror" or even "cabin horror" (Grant, 2014) and how they perpetuate ideas about rural places as dark, sinister, and *scary*. Rural people are portrayed as insular, inbred, cannibalistic monsters who are out to get any outsiders who wander into their remote, isolated territory. In this chapter I examine depictions of rural crime on true crime television for similar stereotypes and imagery. Specifically, I discuss rural true crime storytelling on ID. An examination of ID's substantial true crime offerings reveals that many of ID's original programs feature violent crimes that take place in small-town and rural settings. Shows with titles such as *Murder in the Heartland, Killing Fields, Murder Comes to Town, Welcome to Murdertown, Fear Thy Neighbor, Dead North*, and *Swamp Murders* are a few of the many rural-themed offerings on ID. The names themselves evoke far-off locales where few dare to tread. Similar to the imagery found in backwoods horror movies, the shows' lead-ins, promos, and other visuals showcase dark, spooky forest scenes, run-down houses nestled in wooded lots, weathered barns and sheds, rusted vehicles and farm equipment, barbed wire fences, and lonely dirt roads. These types of images make up what I call the rural-as-scary aesthetic, following my examination of backwoods horror movies, as well as the work of Fulkerson and Lowe (2016), who examined representations of rural in popular U.S. television shows from the 1950s to present. Their analysis found that the predominant TV characterization of rural is one of "morally dangerous, negative, and implicitly inferior" people and places (Fulkerson and Lowe, 2016, p. 32).

I explore the imagery as well as the language used in a sample of these true crime shows for their underlying messages about rurality. I consider

Figure 5.1   Screenshot from the Television Series *Murder Come to Town* **on Investigation Discovery Network.** *Source*: Photograph taken by the author.

why these types of true crime stories are appealing to audiences at this particular period in American history. Using Fulkerson and Thomas's idea of urbanormativity, I examine this true crime TV storytelling and its rural turn as another example of the rural primitive in American popular culture and the role that urbanormativity plays in our popular cultural knowledge base.

True crime has long been a staple in the American television diet. True crime shows such as *Forensic Files*, *Cold Case Files*, and *FBI Files* have drawn large audiences for decades. The forebear of this investigative crime journalism shows, *Unsolved Mysteries*, originally aired in 1987 on NBC, moved to CBS (Columbia Broadcasting System), bounced around to several other networks, and is now syndicated. Netflix rebooted *Unsolved Mysteries* in 2020, and new episodes of the show now appear on the network along with reruns dating back to 1987. Today, all of the major television networks feature some true crime programming—NBC has its long-running *Dateline*, ABC features *20/20*, and CBS offers *48 Hours*. And cable networks now provide new—and nearly continuous—venues for true crime programming. With the proliferation of cable networks, true crime television shows have become a constant presence in U.S. households. Most basic cable networks offer some true crime shows, either original shows or syndicated, previously run programs from other networks. For instance, the Oprah Winfrey Network (OWN) replays episodes of NBC's true crime flagship show, *Dateline*, as well as ABC's *20/20* to round out its original, scripted programming and self-help shows. Similarly, USA Network reruns *Dateline*, as does TLC and Oxygen. The Biography network has its originally run *Killer Kids*; Fox has aired *Cops* since 1989; and several cable networks feature reality shows set in prisons.

TRUE-CRIME-ALL-THE-TIME

Recently, entire cable networks have emerged to zero in on true crime stories. In 2018, the Oxygen Network reorganized and rebranded itself as a
twenty-four-hour true crime network, now calling itself "The *True* Network
for Crime." The emphasis on *true* indicates that the executives at Oxygen
know they have significant competition. That competition comes by way
of ID which arrived at the true-crime-all-the-time playing field first. Owned
by Discovery Channel, ID was founded in 2008 (Steel, 2015). True crime
stories recreated in documentary style comprise ID's inventory. Shows feature interviews with crime survivors, relatives of victims, criminal justice
officials, and journalists involved in the cases. Reenactments with actors in
the style of *Unsolved Mysteries* and crime scene photographs add to the true
crime drama. The network reaches about 1.1 million viewers and is one of the
fastest-growing cable networks (Fernandez and Adalian, 2018; Steel, 2015).
As popular culture writers Maria Elena Fernandez and Josef Adalian observe,
"The boom in crime-driven storytelling on TV at this particular moment is
undeniable" (Fernandez and Adalian, 2018, n.p). If true crime on TV is having a particular moment, then *rural* true crime on TV is having a *particular*
particular moment, especially on the ID network.

ID does run true crime shows that focus on urban crimes—most notably
the show *Homicide City*, which "takes a deep dive into the stories of unfor-
gettable murder from major American cities, as told by veteran detectives
who have seen it all" (https://www.investigationdiscovery.com/tv-shows/ho
micide-city/about). Similarly, ID presents programs highlighting the work of
specific detectives from urban settings, such as *Homicide Hunter* featuring
Detective Joe Kenda of the Colorado Springs, Colorado Police Department
and *Murder Chose Me* with Detective Rod Demery of Shreveport, Louisiana.
And the show *See No Evil* uses surveillance footage to recreate crimes, many
of which take place in cities or large suburbs, where the use of surveillance
cameras is common.

In the late 1980s and the 1990s, fictional crime dramas focused primarily
on urban crimes. Shows like *Law and Order*, *Homicide: Life on the Streets*,
NYPD Blue, *Miami Vice*, *Nash Bridges*, and *The Sopranos* portrayed gritty
urban streets as *the* place of crime. With a few exceptions—such as *Twin
Peaks*, set in a fictional small, Northwestern logging town, and *Murder She
Wrote*, set in rural coastal Maine—television crimes of the 1980s and 1990s
were largely city street crimes. Television news media was (and still is)
urban-centric. As *Time* magazine's Bryan Walsh notes of 1980s Philadelphia,

Blood-soaked local newscasts during the 1980s made it seem as if murder were
Philadelphia's No. 1 product—and the City of Brotherly Love, where homicides peaked at 503 in 1990, was hardly alone in being seen by Americans as

fundamentally unsafe. It was the underlying message of nearly every TV cop show and film thriller made through the 1980s and '90s: The city is dangerous, and you're lucky to get out alive. (2013, n.p.)

This timeframe was at the end of a period that experienced an uptick in the typical street crimes that take place in urban areas, although there was a disproportionate focus on these crimes in the popular news media and fictional crime shows. As Donziger and his coauthors discussed in the 1996 book *The Real War on Crime*, network news, television dramas, and real-life crime-as-entertainment shows stoked a "mean world" syndrome that casts American cities as centers for murder, mayhem, and danger where one was likely to run into a serial killer, a "gang banger," or both, if they ventured down the wrong street (Donziger et al., 1996).

THE RURAL PURGE FROM TELEVISION

The networks' focus on urban crime in the 1980s and 1990s was perhaps not surprising in the context of what some have called television's rural purge (Jicha, 2016; Kaiser and Bernstein, 2014). "Networks in the early 1970s canceled rural-themed shows in favor of a more urban focus" (Belden, 2018, n. p). Hokey, rural-themed comedies such as *The Beverly Hillbillies*, *Green Acres*, *Petticoat Junction*, and *The Andy Griffith Show* were replaced with suburban- and urban-focused fare like the *Brady Bunch*, *All in the Family*, and *Emergency!* (Jicha, 2016).

Karl Jicha's 2016 work outlined the small screen's rural purge of the late 1960s to early 1970s. Around this time, television executives worried about the "viability of rural-themed television programs" (Jicha, 2016, p. 37) and how much advertising revenue they could bring into the networks. Rural shows were still relatively popular; however, they were popular with older, rural viewers. Networks sought a younger, suburban, or urban viewership and their potential advertising dollars. In a short timeframe—from 1969 to 1972—rural shows were all but eliminated from the major networks—especially CBS, which worried about its reputation as the "Country Broadcast System" because it aired several of the popular rural-themed programs (Jicha, 2016; Fulkerson and Lowe, 2016; Kaiser and Bernstein, 2014).

RURAL RETURNS (WITH A VENGEANCE)

Today, however, scripted television shows are looking back at the rural, and often these shows' creators seem to be looking down their noses. As critic Joe Belden states,

A review of many current and recent popular television shows and films seems to show that their network sponsors and city-born-and-raised creators frequently see small towns and rural people as racist, ignorant, pathetic, corrupt, or maybe just viciously murderous and criminal. Examples include critically acclaimed and award-winning TV shows such as *Ozark, Rectify, Sharp Objects,* and *Sons of Anarchy*—as well as the Oscar-winning films *No Country for Old Men* and *Three Billboards Outside Ebbing, Missouri.* . . . A disturbing theme is that *Rectify, Sharp Objects,* and *Three Billboards* all include as a major part of the plot the murder or rape and murder, of teenaged girls, apparently by local folks in each story. (Belden, 2018, n.p.)

HBO's *True Detective,* Season One (2014), set in rural Louisiana, and Season Three (2019), in rural Arkansas, and the recent HBO show *The Outsider* (2020), in rural Georgia, should also be added to Belden's list of TV's rural *noir.*

In the second decade of the new millennium, for true crime television, as with scripted TV shows, a rural turn is afoot. The television gaze has moved beyond urban streets and alleys to rustic dirt roads and cow pastures. This rural true crime trend undoubtedly took hold with the 2015 Netflix documentary series *Making a Murderer,* which follows the homicide case against Steven Avery of Manitowoc County, Wisconsin, a small, working-class farming community. Avery's family live on a property with their sprawling auto salvage business; his family was known to be "all trouble" and "trouble-makers" in the county. The show uses the rural-as-scary aesthetic throughout—foggy dirt roads, dead deer, trailer home after trailer home, and lots of rusted out vehicles (https://www.netflix.com/title/80000770). While this show undoubtedly popularized the rural true crime genre, it was not the first to tap into this TV notion of rural-as-scary. As I will discuss further, the *Murder Comes to Town* series on ID started running in 2014, a year before the release of *Making a Murderer.* To look more closely at this shift to rural locales for true crime on TV, I focus on the ID network and specifically on the *Murder Comes to Town* series. I examine the themes, images, and stereotypes conveyed in rural true crime television and consider why it is so popular at this particular moment.

The ID network is owned by Discovery Inc., a publicly traded company founded by John Hendricks and now run by CEO David Zaslav (https://www.discovery.com/shows). Discovery Channel features many rural-themed reality shows such as *Deadliest Catch, Naked & Afraid, Alaska Bush People, Alaska: The Last Frontier,* and *Gold Rush* (Jicha, 2016). ID was founded in 2008 as an extension of this reality programming and focused solely on true crime (Steel, 2015). Its stock-in-trade is true crime storytelling in the documentary style of *Dateline, NBC,* and *20/20,* with many shows also using the crime scene reenactment method popularized by *Unsolved Mysteries.*

ID shows focus almost entirely on violent crime—mainly murder—and, at first glance, many shows feature small-town and rural crimes, perhaps in keeping with its parent company, Discovery, and its focus on rural reality programming (Jicha, 2016). Titles such as *Murder in the Heartland*, *Hometown Homicide*, *Murder Comes to Town*, *Dead North*, and *Swamp Murders*, to name just a few, evoke images of rural places riddled with homicidal maniacs. Some shows focus on one region or locale, such as *Dead North*: "A true crime thriller set in the Upper Peninsula of Michigan . . . is the story of a female police chief who goes against all odds to uncover what happened on the night Chris Regan went missing" (https://www.investigationdiscovery. com/tv-shows/dead-north/about). Another region-specific show, *Wonderland Murders*, is depicted in this way:

> Once dubbed "Wonderland" because of its immense summer beauty and grandeur, the rolling mountains and deep forests of the Pacific Northwest become a haven for a series of murders. Using stylized re-enactments and interviews with law enforcement personnel and family and friends of victims, episodes focus on a team of dedicated Portland, OR, homicide investigators who seek answers to mysterious, disturbing murder cases. (https://www.investigationdiscovery.com/ tv-shows/the-wonderland-murders)

In this brief description of the show, we see the theme of rural idyll: "Its immense summer beauty and grandeur," turns to rural horror: "A haven for a series of murders."

Still, other rural-themed shows feature a geographic *type* of rural setting, such as ID's *Bloodlands*, set in remote canyon locales, and *Swamp Murders*, about killings that take place in or around low-lying waterways, or in which bodies are dumped in a swamp. These crimes represent events that viewers most likely do not hear about on the nightly news. ID's website touts *Swamp Murders* in this way:

> From the swampy bayou of Louisiana to the Great Lake o' the Cherokees in Missouri, rivers and lakes in Georgia, Texas, and Florida, *Swamp Murders* proves that even muddied waters eventually bring secrets to the surface. . . . Swamps, bogs, marshes, bayous and riverbeds can be murky, dark, crazy places, but when a body pops up, things get downright mysterious. Through stylish recreations, *Swamp Murders* will bring the viewer into the subculture that's captivating America. (https://www.investigationdiscovery.com/tv-shows /swamp-murders/)

How the producers can describe a bunch of disconnected murders throughout the United States as a subculture remains unclear even after viewing numerous episodes of the show. The use of the term "subculture" leads viewers to think that there are certain *kinds* of people *out there*, who commit murders in marshy wetlands as a matter of course.

RURAL-AS-SCARY AESTHETIC ON INVESTIGATION DISCOVERY

From a quick perusal of ID's true crime offerings, it appears as though the network is attempting to capitalize off the rural-as-scary aesthetic. Many of the promotional images on ID use desolate dirt roads, people silhouetted against dimly lit forests, isolated, run-down farmhouses, and other rural-as-scary signifiers. Moving beyond this first impression, to ascertain the urban/rural ratio of true crime shows on ID, I looked at all of its titles, promotional images, and brief descriptions. According to Reelgood, a streaming website and guide that offers TV shows and movies available to stream for free, ID's catalog of original shows numbers at 251, and about 92 of those are currently airing (https://reelgood.com/tv/source/investigation_discovery_go?filter-sort=4). Out of those past and present shows, I tallied forty programs that fit the description of place-based true crime—shows that feature a place in the title, or refer to an area, region, or geographical marker. Three of these titles focused on entire states: *The Golden State Killer* (CA), *Truth is Stranger than Florida*, and *Alaska Haunting*. I eliminated those three from the tally because they may feature both urban and rural locales.

Of the remaining thirty-seven place-based shows, I found twenty-five programs that were *portrayed* as rural. For instance, a show called *Sugar Town* revolves around New Iberia, Louisiana, which ID describes as "a small town with some big problems" (https://www.investigationdiscovery.com/tv-shows/sugar-town/about). According to *World Population Review*, New Iberia's population was almost 30,000 people in 2017, which would better be described as a small city than a small town (http://worldpopulationreview.com/us-cities/new-iberia-la-population/). Nonetheless, ID seems to want to capitalize on the notion of rural-as-scary with both the title and description of *Sugar Town*. To its credit, though, the show is one of the only rural-themed shows I found on ID that addresses racial issues. *Sugar Town* explores the case of a young black man who died in the custody of the county sheriff's department. The death was ruled a suicide despite the fact that the victim was in handcuffs in the back of a police cruiser at the time of his death (D'Alessandro, 2018).

Other shows such as *Murder in the Heartland* focus on the entire Midwest region, but the show's description highlights small towns "rocked by murder." *Murder in the Heartland* is described on ID's website: "Every episode features a town and its people through a murder that tore through it; towns-people become storytellers and hold the clues to the puzzle that has forever changed their lives and how they understand their home" (https://www .investigationdiscovery.com/tv-shows/murder-in-the-heartland/about). This show and other regionally themed rural shows were classified as rural in my sample.

Overall, far fewer of ID's place-based crime shows focus exclusively on urban settings. After tallying up the region of place-based shows on ID, I found that of the ID shows that feature place-based crimes, 68 percent are rural in their descriptions, leaving only 12 percent of programs that focus on a particular urban setting. So, while I was not able to review every one of the 251 shows on the ID network, many of which focus on specific killers, such as various serial killers, or *types* of murderers (women, sisters, twins, the elderly, other family members, neighbors), or murder victims, I did find that *when* focusing on the region or place of crimes, ID looks to rural areas more than it does urban locales. Nearly 70 percent of those shows are rural in their appearance, that is, promotional stills and other graphics, and/or in their descriptions on ID's website. This disparity confirms my initial impression that ID relies on a rural-as-scary aesthetic in its overall programming that centers on the place of crime.

After reviewing all titles on ID and brief descriptions on the website and/ or on IMDb (Internet Movie Database) or Reelgood, I sampled some of the shows that appeared overtly rural. I found that several of these shows *used* rural imagery in the shows' lead-ins and marketing but did not necessarily *focus* on rural crime. For instance, the first episode of *Swamp Murders* I watched featured a female murder victim found in the Merrimack River in Nashua, New Hampshire—the second largest city in the state (by popula-tion). Just as Nashua is not particularly rural, the Merrimack River is not a swamp; it is a major watershed that flows from New Hampshire through northeastern Massachusetts to the Atlantic Ocean. It's nicknamed "The Mighty Merrimack." Similarly, I watched a few episodes of *Wonderland Murders*, and while the show attempts to capitalize on the eerie, dark, forest aesthetic, it centers around Portland, Oregon, homicide detectives. Portland is not rural.

For a closer content analysis of a rural true crime show, I focused on *Murder Comes to Town.* The show is a true crime series that is clearly rural, or as the ID website puts it, the show "reveals what can happen in solitary and desolate places" (https://www.investigationdiscovery.com/tv-shows/mu rder-comes-to-town/about?). *Murder Come to Town* consists of hour-long episodes featuring tales of murder with reenactments and interviews with friends, family, and neighbors of the deceased, along with law enforcement personnel and local journalists. The first episode premiered on January 13,

2014; so far it has run for five seasons, from 2014 to 2018. It has not been renewed for a new season, nor has it been officially canceled by the network (https://www.investigationdiscovery.com/tv-shows/murder-comes-to-town/about). The producers may be beating the rustic, rural bushes for more murders to broadcast on the show.

CONTENT ANALYSIS OF *MURDER COMES TO TOWN*

I selected *Murder Comes to Town* for a close analysis for several reasons. First, the show quite overtly uses the rural-as-scary aesthetic, using urbanormative expectations to appeal to an audience that, producers must assume, do not harken from such out-of-the-way places. The ID website describes *Murder Comes to Town* thusly:

> *Beyond the boundaries of ordinary life,* there is another world that *lies just outside of town,* where *places have no names.* Investigating *forgotten communities past the perimeters* of society, *Murder Comes to Town* reveals what can happen in these *desolate places.* They may be mere minutes from town but *away from civilization, normal rules don't apply and anything can happen.* (emphasis added) (https://www.investigationdiscovery.com/tv-shows/murder-comes-to-town/about)

Urbanormativity runs throughout this description. The city is normal, civilized, inside the bounds of ordinary life. Rural places are "beyond the ordinary," "another world," "past the perimeters," "away from civilization" where "normal rules don't apply" and places "have no names." Notably, after reviewing all episodes of the show, I did not find any unnamed places—all of the townships in the series were named.

Drawing upon language, images, and notions that have been used to label rural populations in the United States for centuries, the *Murder Comes to Town* creators and writers reproduce the long-standing idea that rural people are abnormal, less than; they are *other*. Rural people are described by what they lack: they are *less* civilized, law*less*, their towns *don't even have names*, and *normal rules don't apply* to these remote people. In appealing to a viewer that is presumed to be urban, the show's producers invite "us" to peer in at "them"— their strange ways, their scary habitats, and the violent episodes that define their lives, as far as the show is concerned. This invitation to voyeurism is all the more insidious when you consider that the show is focusing on the worst days of people's lives—the days a loved one or loved ones were murdered.

While the show has aired for five seasons from 2014 through 2018, the stories presented span from the 1990s to the 2000s. Season One included six

Table 5.1   **Regions Represented in MCCT Episodes**

Region	Frequency	Percent
West	6	13.0
Midwest	14	30.4
Northeast	4	8.7
Southwest	2	4.3
South	20	43.4
Total	46	100

episodes; each subsequent season (Two through Five) had ten episodes, for a total of forty-six shows. As table 5.1 illustrates, rural places in the South make up the largest proportion of the episodes at 43 percent. Small towns in Tennessee were featured in five separate episodes and Georgia, Virginian, and Alabama locations were highlighted in three shows each. While the episodes cover all major regions of the United States, overall the show seems to tap into the long tradition of dark, rural Southern gothic tales in its quest to define rural people and places as scary (Murphy, 2013).

Jenny Schuetz of the Brookings Institute recently reviewed the urban versus rural status of scripted television shows in the United States from 1950 to 2017 (2018). She found that most scripted shows take place in real urban settings. Of the scripted shows set in rural places or small towns, more than half are in fictional places (Schuetz, 2018). Historically, the South in particular is underrepresented among scripted shows. As Schuetz found, "The region is home to 37 percent of the nation's people, most of whom don't live in the Baltimore-DC corridor, yet barely registers among scripted shows. Reality TV has embraced all corners of the South, indicating demand for shows in these locations" (Schuetz, 2018, n.p.). *Murder Comes to Town* has indeed embraced the rural South, but in a way that reifies many stereotypes of the people who reside there, they are backward; they are violent; they are insular and isolated.

PERPETRATORS: DO THEY *COME TO* TOWN OR ARE THEY ALREADY THERE?

The show's title would have viewers believe that killers come into these remote settlements from the outside to kill an unsuspecting citizen or citizens. Much of the show's imageries and descriptions, however, seem to rely upon the rural-as-scary notion, wherein the places *themselves* are scary, as are the *inhabitants* who spring forth from these strange locales. So, who are these murderers in the tales told on *Murder Comes to Town*?

The homicides featured on the show are, by and large, relatively typical murders. The victim and the perpetrator are usually family members, romantic partners, friends, or acquaintances. I found very few episodes in which an outsider wanders into a small town and murders a resident. One instance of carnival workers targeting a young mother and her daughter stands apart from the typical domestic violence-related murder. Another episode set in rural Pennsylvania features two drifters who murdered two young adults; this episode also breaks from the pattern. A few episodes featured murderers who were unknown to their victims but were locals or someone from nearby towns. Thus, like most murders in the United States, the murders we see on this rural-themed true crime TV show are committed by people the victims know—and sadly—most often by people they love.

The perpetrators are male—typically young adult white men. In the case of the carnival workers, one of the transient perpetrators was a young white woman, but she was not the main perpetrator; she aided her boyfriend in the crime. Black men committed three out of the forty-six murders on the show; all of those were against black victims. These three shows were the only episodes that featured nonwhite victims or perpetrators. Men comprise the largest proportion of murderers—almost 90 percent—in the United States. Young men under the age of twenty-five make up almost half of all murderers in this country (Seigel, 2015). Statistically speaking, the crimes viewers encounter on *Murder Come to Town* are not unusual crimes.

VICTIMS: RURAL, YOUNG, WHITE, AND FEMALE

The victims featured on *Murder Comes to Town* are only slightly more diverse. A few shows ($N = 3$) highlight mass murders in which an entire family is killed. A handful of victims ($N = 8$) are elderly people, and all but three of those were white. In two of the eight cases with older victims, an elderly couple was killed together. In all eight elder homicide cases, the victims were related to or knew their offenders.

The majority of the cases on *Murder Comes to Town* involve the murders of young, white girls or women. Out of the forty-six episodes, nineteen featured the violent death of one or more white, teenaged, or young adult female. This amounts to 41 percent. Additionally, ten shows involved other white female victims, either middle-aged or elderly people. The show does not always state the ages of the victims or perpetrators, so these ages are estimated based on the descriptions and reenactments. Overall, white females account for 63 percent of all homicide victims on *Murder Comes to Town*. Only three episodes include nonwhite victims, all three were elderly black women and all three were killed by young black males. Further, of those three black male offenders, two were known to the victims and one was hired by the victim's elderly brother in a bid to gain the family inheritance. Therefore,

93 percent of the victims on *Murder Comes to Town* are white. This focus on white female victims corresponds to what scholars of media and crime refer to as the missing (or dead) white woman syndrome (Sommers, 2017; Stillman, 2007) and the news media's attention to young, white female victims who are portrayed as more innocent and therefore more newsworthy (Gilchrist, 2010).

Despite the fact that rural America has experienced a disproportionate amount of opioid and methamphetamine trade, use, and abuse, drugs do not figure prominently in the rural crime stories portrayed on *Murder Comes to Town*. Only a few episodes explicitly involve drugs, at least as the stories are told by the producers of the show. Perhaps rural realities are not as flashy as the notion of either (1) rural townsfolk being killed by strangers who wander into their isolated villages; or (2) rural people killing each other because rural people and places are scary.

Interestingly, not one episode of the show focused on *outsiders entering into* a rural area and being killed *by* rural people—the overriding theme of backwoods horror films. The rural true crime genre seems to want to play off the idea of murderous, territorial rural folk—a theme that is so salient in backwoods horror. But, backwoods horror is fictional. The real crime stories on *Murder Comes to Town* are typical violent crimes—murders by people who know their victims.

Given the fact that all forty-six episodes of the show focus on fairly run-of-the-mill homicides, why the fascination with rural violence? There are several possible answers to that question. The show taps into the rural-as-scary aesthetic for which Americans seem to have a voracious appetite. To understand how this aesthetic runs through this show, I will examine the terms, phrases, sounds, and visual imagery used.

Narration, Words, and Phrases

Murder Comes to Town's narration makes up a big part of its rural-as-scary tone and style. The show was narrated by Joe Alaskey for two seasons until his death in 2017. After Alaskey, Anthony D. Call stepped into the job. Both men use spooky, foreboding intonations to create suspense and intrigue, often accompanied by crows cawing, crickets chirping, or owls hooting. Ominous music plays in the background. The narrators intone clichés like "halfway between neither here nor there suits these Midwesterners just fine" and "in the middle of America and the middle of nowhere," and even "the locals prize their distance *from civilization*." The words and phrases used to describe the rural and small-town settings are similarly hackneyed. Every episode features the narrator saying one or more—usually several—of the following descriptors:

- Wooded
- Small
- Backwoods
- Tiny
- Remote
- Wilderness
- Rural
- Thick woods
- Insular
- Tight-knit
- Mountain—also mountain men and mountain justice
- Lonely
- Desolate
- Farming community
- Backroads

These terms are used repeatedly, with other terms added in for specific areas, such as "dry, eroded" for Montana's landscape.

The phrases, idioms, and clichés used to describe small-town and rural life are also repeated throughout the series. Some variation of "everybody knows everybody" was uttered either by the narrator or a town member in every one of the forty-six episodes, often many times per episode. And, some versions of "everyone knows everyone" hint at extreme insularity and even inbreeding, such as "people who live here go back generations"; and "it's the kind of place where generations can live together for years. . . . I know your grandmother; you know my grandmother." Or, the narrator intones: "They are close-knit people"; or "a lot of folks are kin to each other, if they're not kin, they know each other." While more subtle than the inbreeding themes of the horror films are discussed in chapter 4, the idea of inbreddedness comes through nonetheless.

Another phrase stressed in every episode evoked the notion of community trust. In each and every episode, either a member of the police or sheriff's department, or resident of the town says: "People leave their doors unlocked here," or "Nobody even locks their car doors," or "People leave their keys in their cars." Here the producers seem to want to play up the romantic notions of small-town trust—or what social scientists call collective efficacy—while still using the rural-as-scary idea upon which the show relies.

The narration also highlights just how small and ill-equipped the local police departments are in these remote places and how they must rely on outside authorities to help solve the local homicides. Local sheriffs' departments, or state bureaus of investigations, or the Federal Bureau of Investigation come into town to help local authorities solve the crimes. Over and over again, the show's narrator or the police themselves talk about how understaffed they are and how they are not equipped to deal with major homicide cases.

Imagery

When it is not focusing on a specific location and reenactments, *Murder Comes to Town* uses stock images of rurality. In its lead-ins and before and after commercial breaks, the viewer sees the same images or types of images over and over. The predominant, recurring images are as follows:

- Dirt roads, both dusty and muddy depending on the setting
- Empty fields
- Corn fields
- Crows, both dead and alive
- Weathered barns, sheds, silos, and other farm buildings
- Windmills
- Rusted trucks, cars, and other farm vehicles and equipment
- Trees
- Woods, forests
- Trailer homes in various states of disrepair
- Cabins in woods
- Rolling hills with fog
- Rolling rivers with fog
- Fences—split rail; barbed wire, white picket
- Abandoned store fronts
- Farm animals in pastures—horses and cows
- Hay bales
- Street signs reading "Dead End"

As with the descriptive terms used, while specific images might be chosen to fit a particular setting, such as a foggy forest for a show set in the Pacific Northwest or an arid dirt road for the West, overall, the show's creators use generic, stock photographs or videos of "rural anywhere."

What messages are these repeated images attempting to convey? Clearly, the rural-as-scary is at work here, but what else do the *Murder Comes to Town* viewers learn about rurality? Several themes emerge.

Decay and Decline

Some of the scenes and images shown on *Murder Comes to Town* are beautiful, rural vistas, and some of the show's narration describes the quaintness of these rural outposts. However, the principal scenes of rust, dirt, empty storefronts, weathered buildings, and trailer homes in states of disrepair paint an overall picture of decay—of people and places in states of decline. Images of shuttered storefronts and farming machinery left to rust in the fields hint at the economic hardships that many rural places have experienced in the past several decades, yet the economic issues facing these rural settings are not given much consideration in the tales of murder. Of the episodes in which drugs are mentioned, the hardships of some of the people involved were alluded to, but only in a cursory manner.

Rootedness in Place and Backwardness

As I discussed in chapter 4, rurality and the notion of the rural primitive relies on the idea that people are stuck in time and place—they "go way back" several generations. Residents' grandparents all know one another. Everyone knows everyone because they have all lived in the same place "forever." While "setting down roots" used to be seen as a positive thing to do, this is not the case in rural tales of decline. It is primitive, an anti-modern idea. It flies in the face of progress. Modern societies are mobile societies—you move to where the jobs are, where the action is. The idea of living in the same town as your grandparents runs counter to a modern, urban worldview. *Murder Comes to Town* and other rural true crime shows are yet another recurring reminder that the rural primitive is stuck, rooted, immobile. Rural people can't seem to get out of their own way.

NOT GOING ANYWHERE:
RURAL TRUE CRIME PROLIFERATES ON CABLE TV

The ID network continues to add rural and small-town murder shows to its roster. In late 2019, ID started running *Hometown Homicide: Local Mysteries*, a show that taps the same vein as *When Murder Come to Town*, *Murder in the Heartland*, *Welcome to Murdertown*, and various other shows featuring murders in remote settings. The promos for *Hometown Homicide* look almost identical to *Murder Comes to Town*—dark, foreboding rural scenes interspliced with pictures of cows in fields; voices of local people recount the horrific crimes that took place in their towns.

Other networks, such as twenty-four-hour news networks, are following suit. Headline News (HLN) now airs a series called *Hell in the Heartland*, which follows the general format of ID's *Murder in the Heartland* series. The Travel Channel recently jumped on the rural-as-scary bandwagon with its *Hometown Horror* show featuring local legends and place-based ghost stories found in rural settings. The Travel Channel promotes the show with this description:

> Unassuming American communities are haunted by tales of mysterious, home-grown nightmares. *Hometown Horror* unravels the origins of these frightening stories of the undead, ghouls and monsters lurking in the shadows through eye-witness accounts and historical records. (https://www.travelchannel.com/show s/hometown-horror)

Hometown Horror began in late 2019 and its first season ran episodes on the "Pigman of Angola, New York" (population 2,127 according to the show) and "The Gray People" of Perryville, Kentucky (population of 753 in 2019 according to *World Population Review*), and the "Satanic Swamp" of Freetown, Massachusetts, with its population of about 9,000 (Massachusetts Demographics 2019). While the series does not focus on true crime per se, *Hometown Horror* clearly capitalizes on the rural-as-scary notion and its attendant imagery and tropes. The lead-in image and visual effects for the show are nearly indistinguishable from those of *When Murder Comes to Town*. And, in addition to the "everyone knows everyone" platitude uttered in every episode of *Murder Comes to Town*, residents of these supposedly haunted hometowns inevitably say "everyone in town knows these stories."

Also tapping into the rural-as-scary idea, Oxygen Network—ID's closest competitor—recently released a two-hour documentary entitled "The Piketon Family Murders," recounting the horrific 2016 case of a family of eight who were murdered "execution style" in their beds in four different properties making up a family compound in rural Piketon, Ohio (https://www.oxygen .com/the-piketon-family-murders/season-1/the-piketon-family-murders). The show uses many of the same images and tropes as the rural-themed shows on ID: photographs of run-down barns and trailer homes, dark forests, residents talking about how "everyone knows" or "is related" to everyone in town. America's appetite for rural-as-scary does not seem to be satiated. This particular case received widespread news media attention because it involved a marijuana growth operation and cockfighting on the property. The case went unsolved for two years and is yet to be closed. In 2018, four members of another local family were arrested for the murders. The fact that one of the female victims had a child with one of the male perpetrators added to Hatfield and McCoy nature of this rural crime as well as the public's fascination with it.

SPREADING THE CULTURE OF FEAR BEYOND METROPOLITAN AREAS

In *The Culture of Fear*, Barry Glassner argued that "disproportionate coverage in the news media plainly has an effect on readers and viewers. . . . The leading cause of death, heart disease, received approximately the same amount of [media] coverage as the eleventh-*ranked* cause of death, homicide" (1999, pp. xx–xxi). Further, Glassner states, "From a psychological point of view extreme fear and outrage are often projections" (1999, pp. xxvii). For example, in the 1980s and early 1990s, reports of children being ritually abused by Satanists at daycare sites caused a panic throughout the country. Disproportionate news media coverage of a few reported cases of such abuse grabbed headlines. The fact that many of these cases were baseless and the Satanists involved were never found did not receive much media attention (Glassner, 1999). During this same historical period, American children faced real, tangible dangers: inadequate funding for schools and nutritional programs, lack of housing, lack of affordable and safe daycare, no paid leave for new parents, and lack of access to healthcare and health insurance. These depravities pose much greater danger to children than random bogey-people onto whom we project our fears and blame.

The making of television shows is not innocent or neutral. Just as rural and small-town residents in the 1980s and 1990s who viewed cities through the lens of *Law and Order* and *Homicide: Life on the Streets* might have harbored fear of the urban; the reverse could be true today. City dwellers can hardly be blamed for fearing rurality as they watch the lunatic in Season One of *True Detective* descend upon the detectives with his hatchet and knives, or the murderous redneck families in *Ozark* take out Mexican drug lords without batting an eye. And now U.S. audiences of Investigation Discovery—as well as its audiences in 157 countries and territories (Steel, 2015)—can watch rural true crime stories broadcast into their homes on a seemingly endless loop. These images of the rural primitive on television put rural people at a distance—a safe distance, since they are portrayed as so violent. Ironically, Nic Pizzolatto, one of the creators of *True Detective*, said of rural places in an interview, "These spaces in the country don't get a lot of attention, but that's where the real American story seems to be happening. . . . The crisis of the middle class and its effective dissolution is felt throughout the country, but it is rarely dramatized" (quoted in Derakhshani, 2014, n.p.). While I agree that the problems of the rural poor, working-class, and middle-class families are not often recognized on television, how *True Detective*'s portrayals of homicidal rural primitives help this matter is unclear.

With these TV rural primitives, a population of people continues to be described by what they are not, by what they lack: they are not urban; they are not modern; they lack normal rules; they are beyond civilization. And, as the satanism scare of the 1980s projected a made-up fear onto children who faced real dangers, rural people are lacking, but not in the way these rural true crime shows portray them. They lack employment opportunities; they lack access to healthcare and health insurance; they lack drug rehabilitation programs; they lack access to internet services and public transportation. They lack opportunity. In chapter 6, I consider the effect that the rural primitive in popular culture has on the urban-rural divide, a chasm that will continue to grow if American popular culture focuses on imaginary depravities and not real economic injustices that have disproportionately affected rural areas of the United States.

NOTE

1. An earlier version of this chapter was presented as a roundtable discussion at the 2019 meetings of the American Society of Criminology in San Francisco, CA, at the Marriot Marquis.

Chapter 6

Not So Familiar

Thinking Beyond Rural Stereotypes

Stereotypes of rural people in popular culture, like stereotypes of people everywhere, hinder knowledge and understanding of real people and places. Caricatures of rurality perpetuated in popular culture typically inhabit two ends of a continuum: rural people and places are either (1) simple village folk still living in a romanticized, pastoral idyll (Fulkerson and Thomas, 2019; Jicha, 2016); or (2) inbred, cannibalistic maniacs emerging from the backwoods in horror films. Both of these opposing stereotypes allow rural people and places to be disregarded or seen as scapegoats for larger social ills. In this concluding chapter, I discuss the need to see poor, isolated, rural communities in popular culture without relying on typical rural primitive stereotypes. These rural caricatures divide people across racial lines, class lines, and regional lines. Who benefits from these divisions? While Hollywood continues to make and remake movies about inbred cannibals murdering hapless outsiders, rural inhabitants of the United States are both victims and perpetrators of real crimes—domestic violence, arson, burglaries of farm equipment, drug abuse and addiction. Indeed, the oxycodone scourge in this country began in rural locales and spread into cities and suburbs and is inexorably linked to the opioid abuse crisis now plaguing the entire country. And, apart from crimes, rural residents of the United States also face many other real social problems, such as high suicide rates, increasingly limited access to health care, loss of jobs, homelessness, and environmental hazards, such as those associated with fracking and natural gas extraction, and the dangerous work conditions that come with many rural jobs.

In truly horrifying news, black lung disease—thought to be all but eliminated among coal workers in Appalachia—is on the rise (Bodenhamer, 2020). After the enactment of the Coal Mine Health and Safety Act of 1969, wide-sweeping reforms were put in place to prevent black lung, as well as treat

Figure 6.1   Screenshot of the 2010 movie *Winter's Bone*. *Source*: Photograph taken by author.

and compensate victims whose exposure to coal dust and silica caused this incurable, and often fatal, ailment. The disease is preventable; however, coal companies find ways to avoid protective regulations and make obtaining compensation from the companies and the Black Lung Benefits Trust fund difficult. The recent resurgence of black lung in Kentucky, Virginia, and West Virginia rarely makes the nightly news or even the twenty-four-hour news cycle. Not only is this an example of the types of difficult, dangerous work environments in which rural people labor; the "outlaw operators" (Bodenhamer, 2020) who knowingly cheat the dust sampling systems and put their workers in harm's way provide an example of the types of real rural crimes that escape any recognition—white-collar crimes in rural settings.

Poor, white, rural stereotypes in popular culture must be questioned, critiqued, and hopefully replaced with portrayals of rural places and the people who inhabit them as they are—they can be dark places, but they are not overrun with inbred cannibals. Rural people may seem strange to outsiders, but if you get to know them, they are not as strange as they first appear. The land can be both postcard-esque and foreboding, but to see it as only those two extremes is to miss everything in between.

Fulkerson and Thomas's urbanormativity reveals that rural people are already arranged into a dichotomy with their urban counterparts. Rural stands as the opposite of urban-rural is traditional and archaic where urban is modern and advanced. Rural people are stuck in time and place; they either stay where they are or they even devolve. Urbanites move forward, they progress, evolve. Rural people are primitive; urban people are civilized (Fulkerson and

Table 6.1   The Rural Primitive Dichotomy

Rural as Bucolic, Idyllic	Rural as Scary, Forbidden
• A Getaway from city life	• A dark, untamed place
• A tourist destination	• A wrong turn
• A place to relax, unwind	• A place to fear
• Scenic	• Horrific
• Restorative	• Degraded
• A quaint place	• An unknown place
Romanticizes Rurality	Dehumanizes Rurality

Thomas, 2014, 2016, 2019). The depictions of rural people and places as primitive have become such a mainstay in popular culture that they can also be placed in a dichotomy—some are not as negative as others, but they are all oversimplifications that dehumanize and degrade rurality.

SOMEWHERE BETWEEN RURAL IDYLL AND RURAL HORROR

The two opposing images of rural people—rural idyll versus rural horror—can be seen as counterpoints on a continuum of oversimplifications of rural people—as backward, less than, as primitive (see table 6.1). The primitiveness can be portrayed as quaintness, as in the term "primitive folk art," or it can be represented as savage primitivism, as in "they really went caveman on them," as discussed in chapter 3. Both forms of othering allow urban outsiders to disregard rural people and the challenges they face. They only appear in the media as curiosities or monstrosities, so why should we be concerned about their intergenerational poverty, their loss of hope? They ushered Donald Trump into office, so why should the left care about their tribulations?

CAN WE TALK ABOUT RURAL PEOPLE AND PLACES WITHOUT TALKING ABOUT MONSTERS?

Is it possible to move beyond the strict dichotomies of rural versus urban and rural idyll versus rural horror? Can we talk about rurality in popular culture without talking about rural stereotypes or worse yet, cannibalistic primitives who stopped evolution in their path? It's hard to imagine another group that is depicted in such extreme, dehumanizing ways in mainstream, pop culture. Indeed, filmmaker John Waters once said, "white trash is the last racist thing you can say and get away with" (Wray, 1997, pp. 1–2). I argue you can get away with much more—you can denigrate poor, rural whites to the point of turning them into either caricatures, or worse, inbred monsters.

In American popular culture, rurality is mostly seen as two ends of an opposing spectrum of primitivism, but if we look carefully, we can find some more nuanced images—spaces that open up between rural idyll and rural horror. I found some rural representations in American popular culture where rural people are portrayed in a more nuanced, thoughtful manner. These films and television shows allow viewers to see rural representations as more of a continuum than a strict dichotomy. While these examples may not dismantle the rural stereotypes and exaggerated imagery discussed in this book, they offer a starting point on a path forward.

Brother's Keeper

Brother's Keeper is the story of Delbert Ward of Munnsville, New York (population 499). Delbert is one of four peculiar brothers known in Munnsville as the "Ward boys," despite the fact that the youngest brother is fifty-nine years old when the film begins. The Wards work the dairy farm on which they have lived together as bachelors in the same run-down house for their entire lives. The Wards were always seen as eccentric in the village of Munnsville, but they were part of the small, rural, close-knit, dairy-farming community nonetheless. Delbert's relationship with the rest of the inhabitants of Munnsville changed dramatically after the morning of June 6, 1990, when his brother, William, is found dead in the bed that they shared since they were children. The death is first ruled a natural one, but an autopsy is conducted and the medical examiner decides that William had been deliberately suffocated. The remaining Ward boys are rounded up and taken in for questioning. Later that day, Delbert, who is uneducated and virtually illiterate, *and* without his reading glasses, signs a confession saying he had suffocated his ailing brother as a "mercy killing" since William had been sick.

Documentary filmmakers Joe Berliner and Bruce Sinovsky pick up Delbert's story as his court date is approaching. In the meantime, the inhabitants of Munnsville have rallied around Delbert, taking up collections and raising his $10,000 bail, donating change in coffee cans at the village store, and organizing charity potluck dinner and dances for his lawyer's fees. Most believe he did not kill his brother; others believe he may have killed William, but only to put him out of his misery, which, they say, is a common practice among farmers toward suffering animals. All think he is being framed and unfairly persecuted by the authorities. Delbert's status in the town has moved from curious old-timer to bona fide folk hero, and his murder trial has attracted media attention from all over the state of New York and even the entire country.

The story unfolds as a "city people against rural folk" drama, with undertones of a conspiracy to usurp cheap farmland for development and suburbanization running throughout the town gossip. In this us versus them struggle, Delbert's plight is the townspeople's plight, and if they let the authorities get away with locking Delbert up for murder, they might just be opening the door for further invasions and injustices by these slick outsiders.

The popular media coverage of the case relies on stereotypes of rural farmers as "country bumpkins" and "queer old men living like animals." For instance, Connie Chung comes to town to do a "human interest story" about Delbert. Through Berlinger and Sinovsky's lens, we watch the Ward boys gathered around their television as they watch Ms. Chung characterize them as "primitive" and as "living like farmers did 200 years ago," virtually "without modern farm equipment." Presumably, Ms. Chung didn't make it into the Ward's automated dairy barn. Through their skillful and empathetic documentary, Berlinger and Sinovsky dissect these and other vivid examples of rural stereotypes that infantilize and dehumanize rural people in the maintenance of cultural boundaries between urban "sophisticates" and those "strange country folk." While Munnsville residents view Delbert Ward as merely eccentric or peculiar, the authorities investigating and prosecuting the case and the media representatives who swarm into town regard him as a primitive misfit, especially when the prosecutor floats the idea that the two brothers may have been engaged in incestuous sex at the time of William's death. Berlinger and Sinovsky keep the camera rolling, but in a way that avoids prurient voyeurism. They show the rural residents of Munnsville as they are—they are hardworking; they stick up for their own; they grieve their loved ones; they enjoy each other's company; they stand up for what they believe. Nearly thirty years after its release, the film still stands as a high mark in documentary filmmaking and as a portrayal of a rural place made up of rural people living their lives.

Winter's Bone

The critically acclaimed film *Winter's Bone* (2010, dir. Debra Granik) presents an example of a fictional rural drama that is neither romanticized nor horrific. *Winter's Bone* is based on the 2006 Daniel Woodrell book by the same. Woodrell has lived in the Missouri Ozarks most of his life, and his novels have been described as country noir. The story focuses on Ree Dolly, played by Jennifer Lawrence. Ree is a seventeen-year-old girl trying to keep her family together in the face of extreme poverty in the very rural Missouri Ozarks. The movie paints an unromantic, realistic portrait of a strong female protagonist who is neither the victim nor perpetrator of a bloody crime. She and her family survive by her strength and grit.

Ree sets off on a journey to find her father who has skipped bail on meth-related charges. She faces extreme poverty and potential homelessness with dignity and resourcefulness. Ree is solely responsible for her two younger siblings. Her mother is around physically, but suffers from mental illness and has checked out emotionally. Since Ree's father put the family home up for bail and the bondsman is looking to collect, she must find him, or prove that he is dead. To do so, she must insert herself into the methamphetamine production and distribution scene that lurks in the decrepit barns and shacks that mark the rural countryside. She faces these seemingly insurmountable obstacles with resolve. She has no other choice.

In *Winter's Bone*, race, class, gender, age, and region are explored carefully, thoughtfully. The performances and the movie itself are nuanced, unromantic, and non-stereotypical. Rural women appear as fully fledged, flawed characters, young and old, good and bad. And, like people everywhere, they can be both good and bad. They are fierce and not sexualized. They are cunning and in control as much as they can be in the patriarchal world of the Ozarks and the subculture of rural meth production.

Whiteness, too, is painted in shades we do not typically see on screen. It is not tied to privilege. We see the reality of white intergenerational poverty. The viewer can see that rural poverty is not like urban poverty. If you resort to begging, you are begging from people you know, people you've known your whole life. Rural poverty is stark. Ree must hunt for squirrels and eat pan-fried potatoes day after day because nothing else is available. While the Ozark region is filmed beautifully, there is nothing romantic about this rural landscape. Scenes from the movie evoke a simpler time, but the hardships Ree faces are postmodern in their making: the loss of agricultural jobs with no new jobs to replace them; drugs that have taken hold like the weeds that grow through the floorboards of abandoned meth houses. Yet Ree is not painted as "stuck" in time and place. Yes, she wants to stay in her home; she wants to provide for her young siblings; she does not want to sell their only asset—the beautiful trees on the family land—to pay for her father's misdeeds. But these desires are not portrayed as Ree being stuck or immobile; she loves her home and family and doesn't want to lose them.

In Ree's world, the rural "collective efficacy" and social integration that social scientists like to talk about come with strings attached. A regional code of silence accompanies any generosity Ree receives from neighbors who are slightly better off than her family. Their generosity is also not romanticized— it's delivered with strict warnings attached—the tacit orders to remain silent about her father are made clear to Ree at every point of her rural odyssey. When Ree steps out of line, she receives a beating by other rural women who are doing the bidding for the men. But these same women also protect the young protagonist from the more severe violence that she would no doubt receive at the hands of the men. Just as Granik and author Woodrell dodge rural stereotypes, they also manage to end Ree's rural odyssey on a positive note. Ree's fortitude pays off, and some kindness of others shows through. Even the bail bondsman who had been hounding her shows her some respect and leaves her with not only her home and her woods but also some cash that was put up for bond, most likely by her father's killer.

Frozen River

Frozen River (2008), another movie set in a rural locale, explores similar themes of poverty, lack of opportunity, and female strength. Written and directed by Courtney Hunt, the movie portrays two women—one is Ray (played by Melissa Leo), a white, middle-aged mother of two boys, a teenager, and a five year old. The other is Lila (played by Misty Upham), a Native American young mother of an infant who has been taken from her by her mother-in-law. Both are extremely poor and live on or near the Mohawk Territory in northern New York. Out of desperation, they turn to smuggling immigrants across the frozen St. Lawrence River. Both *Winter's Bone* and *Frozen River* feature women not as part of rural landscapes but as strong protagonists in command of their own stories. The filmmakers draw the characters as brave, resourceful, and fully human. The women make some not-so-great choices in a strict economy of frozen rural choices. Hunt, the director of *Frozen River*, gets the details of a rural economy right; for instance, the white woman works at the "Yankee One Dollar" a stand-in for the Dollar General stores that have cropped up in rural locales across the United States. The number of Dollar General stores reached about 30,000 in 2020, and all are located in areas described as places where "a permanent underclass" resides (Edelman, 2020). And the only place for people to meet socially is a bingo hall where meager earnings grow even more meager.

Desperation leads the women to their unlikely friendship and their illegal activity. Like the protagonist in *Winter's Bone*, both Ray and Lila strengthen their resolve and do what they need to do to keep their families together. The movie is unsentimental, bleak—set on a frozen landscape where the rural poor, especially rural poor women, are frozen out of opportunities. It tackles several everyday realities affecting residents of this part of the country: illegal immigration, racism, grinding poverty, gambling, foreclosures, and repossessed trailer homes. The fear of cracking ice stands as a constant reminder of the tenuous existences these women live. The interracial friendship represents a positive theme and ends on an encouraging note, however. In their stark realism, both *Winter's Bone* and *Frozen River* come close to the edge of hopelessness but pull back just enough to offer some hope—hope that rural places, like these resilient rural women, can survive.

Justified: Rural Crime on Television that Resists Caricature

I have found a few places on the small screen where viewers can see some examples of more nuanced images of rural people and places. *Justified*, a rural crime series that ran on the FX network for six seasons, 2010–2015, offers one such place. *Justified*, set in Harlan County, Kentucky, manages to resist most of the more blatant stereotypes about Appalachia. As one critic said of the show, "Perhaps the thing I like most about *Justified* is its honest and unapologetic depiction of the rural lifestyle . . . the show depicts some of the issues that real people face on a daily basis, but never deriding or judging its setting or characters as more mainstream depictions often want to do" (Crider, 2011, n.p.). Where most TV rural criminals are depicted as one-dimensional characters at best and grotesque caricatures at worst, *Justified* offers a multidimensional view of rural people and the crimes they commit or fight. The show avoids hillbilly, mountain men stereotypes, and it illustrates that crimes should be understood within their social, cultural, and historical contexts. The show humanizes people who are often portrayed as less than human or drawn as dumb, toothless, and inbred.

Based on *Fire in the Hole*, a novella by Elmore Leonard (2002) and set in Harlan County and Lexington, Kentucky, the show stars Timothy Olyphant as Deputy U.S. Marshal Raylan Givens. Raylan grew up in Harlan County and returns as a marshal reassigned to Lexington after killing a man in Florida, point-blank and in the middle of a restaurant. But, as he reminds anyone who brings it up, the other guy drew first, making the killing justified. The show also stars Walton Goggins as Boyd Crowder: outlaw, former white supremacist, backwoods preacher, and Raylan's childhood friend and alter ego. Raylan and Boyd are drawn as two sides of the same coin. They take turns as protagonist and nemesis, friend and foe. *Justified* does not offer simple storylines of good battling evil—both of the main characters, as well as many of the show's other characters, embody good and bad. They also carry a long history of illegal activities in the remote landscape—modes of adaptation to the remoteness and isolation of the hills and hollers. Moonshine has been replaced by marijuana, methamphetamine, and "pills"—oxycontin.

The second season of the show features two feuding families who finally collide. While the idea that the Appalachian Mountains are filled with feuding families hews close to stereotype, the writers avoid oversimplification. The show draws upon Appalachian history without belittling it. In fact, the writers appear to draw from the documentary, *Harlan County, USA*, the 1976 Academy Award-winning documentary by Barbara Kopple. *Harlan County, USA* follows the coal miners' strike against the Duke Power Company for better wages and safer working conditions. The film features rural Appalachian folk hero and labor organizer Florence Reese. Reese addressed a crowd with her famous song, "Which Side Are You On?" She wrote the song during an earlier Harlan County coal strike in 1931.

Reece's activism is alluded to in Season Two of *Justified* when a sixty-something Appalachian matriarch known as Mags (played by Margo Martindale) gives a rousing speech at a town hall meeting. Mags speaks forcefully against a mining company that wants to strip the top off of the local mountain to extract the coal inside. Mags defends her holler against this outside force who will not only extract the natural resources but also pollute the area with the run-off from the mines. Yet Mags is no hero; she is no Florence Reece. She was actually buying up local property to sell to the mining company, double-crossing her neighbors and family members alike. While she seems fiercely protective of her adult children—her boys—she also brutally assaults one with a hammer. She takes in a neighbor's daughter, but only after she killed the girl's father for growing marijuana on his property. She wants to corner that market.

Justified is by no means perfect; it dances around hillbilly stereotypes, but it also represents rural people in more subtle ways than typically seen on television. The showrunners know the history of the region and the actors work against stereotype. In an interview with *The New York Times*, Walton Goggins, who played Boyd Crowder, said his character was initially presented to him as a stereotypical "over-the-top redneck racist" in the pilot. But he said, "I wasn't interested in playing that person. . . . I'm from the South—I'm not going to sell out my own culture for the sake of a television show" (Egner, 2011, AR14).

MAYBE PARODYING WILL HELP

Humor provides a tool to diffuse stereotypes and turn age-old assumptions on their heads. The inbred horror movie tropes have grown so common that they are now being parodied in film. The horror genre has become a venue for satire and commentaries on assumptions about race, class, and gender (Hayden, 2016; DeKeseredy et al., 2014; Boger, 2018; Clover, 1992). Horror films tend to be a devalued art form, making them a powerful vehicle to debunk myths about devalued people. And, when the grotesque stereotypes about horrific inbred mountain men are parodied from within the genre, these parodies are all the more powerful.

As I discussed in chapter 4, *Tucker & Dale vs. Evil* (2012) represents an example of a film that turns these "backwoods folks are inbred monsters" tropes on their heads. Like so many of the backwoods horror films before it, the film is set in the Appalachian Mountains in West Virginia. Inverting the scary, rural, inbred white male monster stereotype, the film introduces viewers to two harmless, kind-hearted, rural young men—locals—who buy an old shack in the middle of the woods to fix up as a retreat for fishing. They have jobs in town, but they want a retreat to spend some quality time in the pastoral (not scary), wooded setting. As in every backwoods horror film, the local men, Tucker and Dale (played by Alan Tudyk and Tyler Labine), are met by a group of college students who immediately size up the two locals as strange, peculiar—as other. As in the first *Wrong Turn* movie and countless other backwoods horror films, this first encounter takes place in the local county-store-gas-station-bait shop.

Later that evening, the "college kids" (as Tucker and Dale call them) stay up late telling scary stories of bygone college students who, while on a Memorial Day outing twenty years earlier, are murdered by the locals. In the *Tucker & Dale* plot, though, the college students are so hapless that they seem to be throwing themselves into harm's way while in the vicinity of Tucker and Dale. Inverting the scary backwoods man stereotype, the two locals try to help these accident-prone youths. They come to the aid of a young female co-ed, Allison, who fell into the water near their fishing boat, bringing her to their cabin so she can recuperate, as her friends appear to have abandoned her. Her friends, of course, think the protagonists have brought her there to cannibalize her, just like the locals do in all of the backwoods horror films (Hayden, 2016). As the story progresses, we learn more about the kindness of the two local men. Playing with both the rural as simple trope and the rural as horrific trope, director Eli Craig depicts Dale in particular as gentle, romantic, and protective of the outsider in their midst. Dale is the sympathetic focal point of the movie, and unlike the horror films it spoofs, the audience roots for this gentle giant of the West Virginia mountains. The friendship between the two protagonists makes them both sympathetic. Here, we see two non-related rural men who care for one another and cheer each other on in the face of danger and confusion.

As the movie progresses, more of the college students get killed off by their own haplessness and reliance on stereotypes. For instance, one college guy runs into a tree, impaling himself with a branch because he sees Tucker waving around a chainsaw. What the outsider doesn't see is that Tucker ran into a bees' nest. As he waves his implement around, he looks every bit like Leatherface from *The Texas Chainsaw Massacre*—a character that is so recognizable; he needs no further introduction. The entire movie follows this narrative of Tucker and Dale trying to help the helpless college kids, but all the while appearing to the college kids as though they are "out to get them" (Hayden, 2016). The film plays with the backwoods horror staple of outsiders trespassing on local property, as Dale remarks, "Kids just started killing themselves all over my property!" Tucker agrees, saying, "It's a suicide pact!"

Finally, the plot twists to reveal that one of the college kids is the bad guy—a guy named Chad who pops the collar of his polo shirt and is a member of a fraternity. In one of the final scenes, Dale saves Allison (the "last girl" left, see Clover, 1992) from Chad, shouting, "You want a killer hillbilly; I'll show you a killer hillbilly. . . . Bring it frat bitch!" The film subverts assumptions about class, whiteness, and masculinity in an over-the-top send-up of the entire genre of backwoods horror. There is even a nod to the movie *Fargo* when another unfortunate college kid runs headlong into a wood-chipper that Tucker uses to clear the overgrown area around the cabin. The notion that the two "mountain men" are tidying up their forest retreat works against a basic premise of hillbilly horror—the idea that the inbred rural people are part of their overgrown, dark, forbidden surroundings. They are supposed to lurk in the woods, not clear the trees for better visibility. Throughout the film, the typical imagery found in *Wrong Turn* films and their ilk is present, but they are not scary. We see trees, flannel, bib overalls, hatchets, scythes, chainsaws, pickup trucks, and woodchippers; but they are presented as normal, not as harbingers of violence. These are clothing people wear, tools people use. In an interview with the horror blog Horrorbid, the film's director Eli Craig says, "It's a film that sticks up for the humanity of rural redneck folks against the collar-popping kids . . . we had the actors watch Wrong Turn, The Hills Have Eyes, and Texas Chainsaw Massacre so the kids they could play to stereotypes" (*Horrorbid*, 2011). The film succeeds in upending the all-too-familiar tropes of rural places as scary and rural people as grotesque homicidal maniacs.

A similar, although less thorough, parody is presented in the comedy film *Harold and Kumar Go to White Castle* sequel, titled *Harold and Kumar Escape from Guantanamo Bay* (2008). The film features a sequence in which the protagonists stumble upon a backwoods scene that inverts many hillbilly horror stereotypes. The two main characters—lost in a wooded area—meet up with a grotesque looking man in a tow truck. His name is "freakshow," and his face is disfigured with seeping sores. He sings hymns and asks if they have accepted Jesus into their lives. He takes them to his home, a trailer in the middle of the woods. They meet his wife. The backwoods people are helpful and hospitable; their trailer is neat as a pin; the man of the house is a fastidious clean freak (Hayden, 2016). The inbred stereotype rears its ugly head, however, when Harold and Kumar stumble upon the couple's cycloptic son who was hidden in the basement. Here, however, the supposedly inbred boy—the cyclops— serves to illustrate how ridiculous the inbred monster stereotypes are, which is certainly a step forward in the popular imagery of the rural (Hayden, 2016).

Rural Parody on Television

The cult hit television show *Schitt's Creek* provides another example of rural imagery that satirizes rural stereotypes—both dancing around them and even embracing them to illustrate just how wrong-headed they are. While *Schitt's Creek* is a Canadian show set in rural parts of Ontario, the show's creators were careful to not identify the actual setting of the show—the idea is that it could be any rural place in North America (Lawson, 2019; Patrick, 2018). Indeed, the characters mention having previously lived in both the United States and Canada. The rural settings for the episodes do not reveal any clear markers of location—no street signs or flags can be seen. This increases the show's broad appeal; the small town is an allegory for rural, isolated, far away. It also makes the characters feel truly stuck in Schitt's Creek.

Schitt's Creek turns the Beverly Hillbillies conceit on its head. The very wealthy Rose family—father Johnny, mother Moira (both in their sixties), adult son David (in his early thirties), and adult daughter Alexis (early twenties)—fall on hard times. Everything they own—mansion, furniture, cars, designer cloths, and handbags—is seized by the government due to some vague malfeasance by Johnny's business partner as well as the family's own spending habits. The only property they still own is the rural town of Schitt's Creek, which Johnny purchased in the early 1990s as a joke for David. The family relocates from their extravagant surroundings and lands in Schitt's Creek where they take up residence in a run-down motel.

Unlike the horror parodies, Schitt's Creek skewers the other end of the rural primitive continuum—the rural as quaint, bucolic. It is a simple place seemingly populated by simple people. The Rose family retreats to this small-town outpost, and at first, they look down on the rubes they encounter. The show is now in its sixth season (2015–2020), and after the initial encounters between the newcomers and natives in the first season or so, the Roses adapt. Instead of trying to claw their way back to the rat race they came from, the family begins to see the benefits of this rural existence where "everyone knows everyone." They start their own small businesses and contribute to the small-town economy; they join theater and singing groups. David even hunts with his new friends. Both adult children fall in love with people in their rural outpost, but never quite leave their parents' nest in the motel. The family learns to be a family. The show succeeds in *parodying* quaintness while at the same time *being quaint*.

Schitt's Creek is lauded by critics for many of its positive portrayals—of pansexuality, of the strength of family and community, and its overall comedy writing and acting. From an urbanormative perspective, it also works toward highlighting some of the assumptions we make about the urban-rural divide. It pokes fun at all sorts of divisions: between rich and poor, between urban and rural, between rootlessness and rootedness. What the show does best is play with contrasts between a wealthy, urban mindset with all its capitalist trappings versus the appeal of a small-town community with its seemingly "quaint" and "simple" and even "peculiar" ways. As the Rose family starts to identify with their rural community, so too does the audience, thereby humanizing the rural other. And, in turn, the small town changes with the presence of the Roses. They start to adopt some of their cosmopolitan views about theater, music, and film.

FINAL THOUGHTS: BETTER REPRESENTING RURAL

Ernest Hebert, a novelist who centers much of his writing in the Monadnock region of New Hampshire, wrote a series of novels about a kinship network that could be labeled an "inbred community" made up of rural primitives. The series, known as the Darby Chronicles, paints an alternative view of remote, isolated people and places—an antidote for the rural primitive. The Darby Chronicles includes seven novels spanning thirty-five years in the life of a small, rural New England town. Three families make up the cast of characters—the Elmans, the Salmons, and the Jordans—and each represents a social class.

In an essay titled "People of the Kinship," which was included in a reprint of two of his novels from the Darby Chronicles, *A Little More than Kin* and *The Passion of Estelle Jordan* (1993), Hebert describes his approach to writing about rural places and people:

> When I created the Jordan clan in the first novel if the Darby Series, *The Dogs of March*, I called them "the Shack People." They were based on men, women and children I'd grown up with in Keene and in the surrounding towns of Cheshire County. Our New England forest is messy and crowded, just like the Jordan shacks. I postulated a connection between the landscape and people who by necessity live close to the earth. Maybe so, but since driving across the United States a number of times, I've been amazed to find Jordan shacks all over the country. I am now convinced that a libido for shack-living is based more in culture than in topography. . . . What the motorist sees of the Shack People from the road is disheveled housing, dogs in the yard, an in-bred look to the people . . . know them better and you learn that they distrust authority outside their clans and possess a contemptuous attitude toward education, success, law, and indeed toward what most of us would call our values. You also realize that they're no smarter or stupider than anybody else. They just have different priorities. (1993, pp. 4–5)

Hebert's novels articulate his ability to discuss poor, clannish, even incestuous, groups in a way that does not romanticize nor mythologize but, most importantly, maintains their humanity. The very fact that he places the Jordan family, whom he calls the clan, at the center of this series, and not the periphery, is remarkable. They are not lurking in the background, nor are they monsters; they are not quaint or horrific.

In the following passage from *A Little More than Kin* (1993), the author describes a scene in which Howard Elman searches the woods for Ollie and Willow Jordan. Howard is not a member of the Jordan clan, but he is a friend of Ollie Jordan, the father of a father-son pair. Ollie's son, Willow, is a young man in his early twenties with some developmental problems. The story earlier revealed that the father and son are also brothers, born to the same mother. This revelation is brought to light without any stomach-turning imagery or tawdry punch lines, and no clear causality is drawn between Willow's inbrededness and his mental problems, which his father views only as peculiarities. The father and son had taken to the woods when the "Welfare Department" (social services) threatened to take Willow away. They assume he will be institutionalized—removed from the only place he knows. Howard Elman eventually finds them. Hebert writes:

He found Ollie and Willow beside a tree. The snow had covered their bodies, but Ollie's face was visible. The eyes were closed, the expression placid, the skin deep blue . . . the boy was naked in his father's arms. They were half-sitting, half-reclining, as if on a chaise lounge. They were frozen solid, interwound so they could not be separated. Blue statues formed by some master craftsmen. They were beautiful.

Elman sat down on a log to smoke a cigarette. He didn't know what to do next. By law, he should walk down the mountain, call the cops, and lead them back up here. But he knew Ollie hated the authorities and would not want his body or the body of his son in their hands. Elman imagined Godfrey Perkins, the town constable, spreading it all over Darby that Willow had been found bareass in his father's embrace. He would make a dirty thing of it. . . . Elman believed he had to give these bodies a dignified resting place. He touched them. They were as hard as stone, even the eyelids. It would be easier to move them one at a time, but difficult to chisel them free from one another without damaging them. He decided to move them as one. . . . "Chains of being" he called them. The idea of chains of being thrilled Elman and triggered something in his mind, and he was seeing Willow doing some stupid-ass thing and hearing Ollie saying, "My, what a sense of humor that boy has got," and his knowledge of the Jordans came together. In a moment, he understood the kind of love that had welded Ollie and Willow. (1993, pp. 213–214, 217)

In this passage, as in the novel and the entire series, Hebert is able to describe members of a poor, inbred, pariah community without relying on typical white trash stereotypes, lurid scenes of incestuous rape, or grotesque images of genetically mutated monsters. Ollie and Willow do share the same body, but this is not grotesque, it's even beautiful. They are over-related, as connected as links in a chain, but the reader is not nudged toward primitive horror—it is a picture of familiarity, not disgust (Hayden, 1997). In his essay about how he approached his depictions of the Jordans, Hebert noted that these groups, when portrayed in fiction, "if they were portrayed at all, often came off as unreal. For example, even a good writer such as James Dickey writing a good book, *Deliverance*, reduced Shack people to the level of subhumans with not a whisper of complaints from critics or public" (1993, p. 11). Hebert also recognizes:

> The Shack People are the most despised and least understood of Americans, because, I believe, we in mainstream America define ourselves in opposition to them. Good teeth, clean bodies, tidy houses, spacious lawns and specious virtues are not only traits of the American character, they're national fetishes. . . . Good learning and good manners might aid one's advancement in American society, but good teeth, a clean body, and passable stylishness are requirements. At this time, we fishes in the mainstream are wearing wild ties, listening to rap music and debating multiculturalism. The Shack People are . . . oblivious to us and out "new" ideas. (1993, p. 6)

I have spent some time discussing Hebert's work here because his writing stands as an exemplar for presenting rural places and the people who inhabit them in a way that is not so familiar. He recognizes that much of what we consume about rurality in popular culture comes from an urbanormative perspective that views rural as abnormal, strange, and less than civilized. As someone who grew up in rural New England and who took the time to get to know rural people, he offers a alternative approach that recognizes their differences but does not demean them and place them on a lower rung of the evolutionary ladder.

All of the films, television shows, and literature discussed in this chapter provide some reason for optimism around popular cultural images of rural people and places.

Can these images counter the prevailing views of rurality? Will these images and literature change long-held rural stereotypes? As Fulkerson and Thomas discuss in the conclusion to their edited volume, *Reimagining Rural: Urbanormative Portrayals of Rural Life* (2016), as social norms shift, tolerance of biased media representations fall away. And vice versa: as stereotypical media portrayals of rural people become less visible, urbanormative standards about rurality will also fade. The current sociocultural imagination is still rife with stereotypes, but it is also becoming increasingly apparent that some artists are willing to illustrate how silly and demeaning those depictions are. This reclamation process is ongoing, as it is with all marginalized groups. African Americans continue to fight stereotypes of their community through films, literature, music, parody, and satire. And they continue to be confronted with more and more cultural appropriation of their art, their hairstyles, their music, and their language. If it's not being denigrated, their culture is being co-opted by wealthy whites.

The same trend can be seen at the corners of popular culture with the appropriation of so-called white trash culture on film and in fashion and music. In an essay titled "What's the Deal with Justin Bieber and Post Malone's white trash Aesthetic?" cultural critic Emma Madden (2018) comments on this emerging trend—a trend consisting of "codified grubbiness," Joe Dirt moustaches, Hawaiian shirts, bandanas, and trailer homes (2018). As Madden states, "Its aesthetic is hyper-visual, with Hawaiian shirts and pink flamingos and bellies that crash into each other like bumper cars. Whites have been described as the 'invisible race,' but white trash make their adversity remarkably apparent" (2018, n.p.). Similarly, Beyoncé, Nicki Minaj, and Taylor Swift have all recently released music videos set in trailer parks. Appropriating other groups' cultures is not a new trend, but wealthy white artists co-opting poor whites' aesthetic does add a new twist. Is it a step toward normalizing rurality? Is it a form of appreciation that might lead to acceptance? Perhaps. But the history of cultural appropriation doesn't suggest that will be the case any time soon.

Plenty of academic work and cultural critique still needs to be done on popular imagery of rural people and places. Further examinations are needed into the areas where rurality is discussed in ways that are not stereotypical, as with the realist films discussed in this chapter, or in ways that parody or spoof those age old stereotypes, as in the horror comedy film *Tucker and Dale vs. Evil* and the television show *Schitt's Creek*. These mediums cannot dismantle centuries of rural primitive myths overnight, but they are slowly chipping away at our urbanormative assumptions. These projects can open up more room for academic projects that both humanize rural others and examine the actual hardships they face.

References

Anderson, N. F. (1986). Cousin marriage in Victorian England. *Journal of Family History* 11, 285–301.

Arens, W. (1986). *The Original Sin: Incest and Its Meaning.* New York: Oxford University Press.

Belden, J. (2018). Speak Your Piece: Hollywood's Rural America is a Scary Place. *The Daily Yonder: Keep It Rural.* https://dailyyonder.com/speak-piece-hollywoods -rural-america-scary-place/2018/09/07/. Accessed on September 7, 2018.

Bell, D. (1997). Anti-idyll: Rural horror. In: Cloke, P. and Little, J. (eds.), *Contested Countryside Cultures: Otherness, Marginality, and Rurality*, pp. 94–108. New York: Routledge.

Bodenhamer, A. A. (2020). 'Outlaw operators': Prevention failures and the resurgence of black lung in central Appalachia. *Carsey Institute National News Brief* 149, 1–6.

Boehrer, B. T. (1992). *Monarchy and Incest in Renaissance England: Literature, Culture, Kinship, and Kingship.* Philadelphia, PA: Temple University Press.

Boger, J. (2018). Manipulations of stereotypes and horror clichés to criticize post-racial White liberalism in Jordan Peele's *Get Out. The Graduate Review* 3 (22), 149–158.

Carlson, E. T. (1985). Medicine and degeneration: Theory and praxis. In: J. E. Chamberlin and S. L. Gilman. (eds.), *Degeneration: The Dark Side of Progress*, pp. 121–144. New York: Columbia University Press.

Chamberlin, J. E. (1985). Images of degeneration: Turnings and transformations. In: J. E. Chamberlin and Gilman, S. L. (eds.), *Degeneration: The Dark Side of Progress*, pp. 263–289. New York: Columbia University Press.

Chamberlin, J. E. and Gilman, S. L. (1985). Degeneration: An introduction. In *Degeneration: The Dark Side of Progress.* New York: Columbia University Press.

Clifford, James. (1986). "On ethnographic allegory." In: Clifford, J. and Marcus, G. E. Marcus (eds.), *Writing Culture: The Poetics and Politics of Ethnography,* pp. 98–121. Berkeley, CA: University of California Press.

Cloke, P. and Little, J. (1997). *Contested Countryside Cultures: Otherness, Marginality, and Rurality*. New York: Routledge.

Clover, C. J. (1992). *Men, Women, and Chainsaws: Gender in the Modern Horror Film*. Princeton, NJ: Princeton University Press.

Cooley, W. C., Rawnsley E., Melkonian, G. Moses, C. McCann, D., Virgin, b, Coughlan, J. and Moeschler, J. B. (1990). "Autosomal dominant familial spastic paraplegia: Report of a large New England family." *Clinical Genetics* 38, 57–68.

Crider, M. (2011). 'Justified' Season 2 Finale Review and Discussion. *Screenrant*. https://screenrant.com/justified-season-2-finale-review-discussion/.

D'Alessandro, A. (2018). Sugar Town: ID Doc Explores Injustice in a Handcuffed Black Youth's Death. Retrieved from https://deadline.com/2018/07/sugar-town-investigation-discovery-doc-explores-injustice-in-handcuffed-black-youths-death-tca-1202434648/. Accessed on July 26, 2018.

Darwin, C. (1858). *The Origin of Species*. London: John Murray.

———. ([1871] 1874). *The Descent of Man: Selection in Relation to Sex*. New York: A. L. Burt, Publisher.

———. (1871, 1877). *Various Contrivances by Which Orchids are Fertilized*, 1st and 2nd editions. New York: Appleton.

Davies, C. (1982). Sexual taboos and social boundaries." *American Journal of Sociology* 87, 1032–1063.

Degler, C. N. (1991). *In Search of Human Nature: The Decline and Revival of Darwinism in American Thought*. New York: Oxford University Press.

DeKeseredy, W. S., Muzzatti, S. L. and Donnermeyer, J. F. (2014). Mad men in bib overalls: Media's horrification and pornification of rural culture. *Critical Criminology* 22, 179–197.

Derakhshani, T. (2014). Cable Crime Shows Explore Rural America's Underbelly. *Philadelphia Inquirer*. Retrieved from https://www.seattletimes.com/entertainme nt/cable-crime-shows-explore-rural-americarsquos-underbelly/. Accessed on February 27, 2014.

Dickey, James. (1970). *Deliverance*. New York: Bantam Doubleday, Dell Publishing Group, Inc.

Discovery, Inc. http://www.discovery.com/shows.

Donnermeyer, J. F. and DeKeseredy, W. S. (2014). *Rural Criminology*. New York: Routledge.

Donziger, S. A. (1996). *The Real War on Crime: The Report of the National Criminal Justice Commission*. New York: Harper Collins.

Douglas, M. (1966). *Purity and Danger: An Analysis of the Concepts of Pollution and Taboo*. New York: Routledge.

Dugdale, R. L. ([1887] 1910). *The Jukes: A Study in Crime, Pauperism, Disease, and Heredity*, 4th edition. New York: G. P. Putnam's Sons.

Durkheim, E. ([1933] 1964). *The Division of Labor in Society*. New York: The Free Press.

Edelman, M. (2020). How Capitalism Underdeveloped Rural America. *Jacobin Magazine*. https://jacobinmag.com/2020/01/capitalism-underdeveloped-rural-am erica-trump-white-working-class. Accessed on January 26, 2020.

Egner, J. (2011). A son of the South with many accents. *The New York Times*. p. AR14.

Elias, N. ([1939] 1978). *The Civilizing Process, vol. 1: The History of Manners*. Oxford: Basil Blackwell.

Farber, B. (1972). *Guardians of Virtue: Salem Families in 1800*. New York: Basic Books.

Fernandez, M. E. and Adalian, J. (2018). How TV's Biggest True-Crime Players Find Their Stories. Retrieved from https://www.vulture.com/2018/07/tv-true-crime -networks-how-they-find-their-stories.html.

Foucault, M. (1978). *The History of Sexuality: An Introduction, vol. 1*. New York: Vintage.

Fox, R. (1983). *The Red Lamp of Incest*. New York: E. P. Dutton.

Fulkerson, G. M. and Lowe, B. (2016). Representations of rural in popular North American television. In: Fulkerson, G. M. and Thomas, A. R. (eds.), *Reimaging Rural: Urbanormative Portrayals of Rural Life*, pp. 9–34. Lanham, MD: Lexington Books.

Fulkerson, G. M. and Thomas, A. R. (2014). *Studies in Urbanormativity: Rural Community in Urban Society*. Lanham, MD: Lexington Books.

———. (2019). *Urbanormativity: Reality, Representation, and Everyday Life*. Lanham, MD: Lexington Books.

———. (2016). *Reimagining Rural: Urbanormative Portrayals of Rural Life*. Lanham, MD: Lexington Books.

Genge, N. E. (1995). *The Unofficial X-Files Companion*. New York: Crown Trade Paperbacks.

Gilchrist, K. (2010). "Newsworthy" victims: Exploring differences in Canadian local press coverage of missing/murdered Aboriginal and White women. *Feminist Media Studies* 10 (4), 373–390.

Gilman, S. (1985). Sexology, psychoanalysis, and degeneration: From a theory of race to a race to theory." In: Chamberlin, J. E. and Gilman, S. (eds.), *Degeneration: The Dark Side of Progress*, pp. 72–69. New York: Columbia University Press.

Glassner, B. (1999). *The Culture of Fear: Why Americans are Afraid of the Wrong Things*. New York: Basic Books.

Goad, J. (1997). *The Redneck Manifesto: How Hillbillies, Hicks, and White Trash Became America's Scapegoats*. New York: Touchstone.

González-López, G. (2015). *Family Secrets: Stories of Incest and Sexual Violence in Mexico*. New York: New York University Press.

Gough, R. J. (1989). Close-kin marriage and upper-class formation in late eighteenth century Philadelphia. *Journal of Family History* 14, 119–136.

Grant, M. (2014). The cabin on the screen: Defining the "cabin horror" film. *Film Matters* 2014, 5–12.

Greenslade, W. (1994). *Degeneration, Culture, and the Novel, 1880–1940*. New York: Cambridge University Press.

Greven, D. (2019). Review of Robin Wood on the horror film: Collected essays and reviews. *Cineaste* XLIV (3), 1–6.

Groce, Nora Ellen. (1985). *Everyone Here Spoke Sign Language: Hereditary Deafness on Martha's Vineyard.* Cambridge, MA: Harvard University Press.

Grossberg, M. (1985). *Governing the Hearth: Law and Family in Nineteenth Century America.* Chapel Hill, NC: University of North Carolina Press.

Hall, P. K. (1977). Family structure and economic organization: Massachusetts merchants, 1700-1850. In: Hareven, T. (ed.), *Family and Kin in Urban Communities, 1700–1950*, pp. 36–61. New York: Viewpoints.

Harper, P. and D. F. Roberts. (1988). Mating patterns and genetic disease." In: Mascie-Taylor, C. G. N. and Boyce, A. J. (eds.), *Human Mating Patterns*, pp. 169–181. Cambridge: Cambridge University Press.

Hayden, K. (2016). Inbred horror revisited: The fear of the rural in twenty-first century backwoods horror films. In: Fulkerson, G. M. and Thomas, A. R. (eds.), *Reimagining Rural: Urbanormative Portrayals of Rural Life*, pp. 59–72. Lanham, MD: Lexington Books.

———. (2014a). Inbred horror: Degeneracy, revulsion, and the fear of the rural community. In: Fulkerson, G. M. and Thomas, A. R. (eds.), *Studies in Urbanormativity: Rural Community in Urban Society*, pp. 181–205. Lanham, MD: Lexington Books.

———. (2014b). Stigma, reputation, and place structuration in a coastal New England town." In: Fulkerson, G. M. and Thomas, A. R. (eds.), *Studies in Urbanormativity: Rural Community in Urban Society*, pp. 67–85. Lanham, MD: Lexington Books.

———. (1997). *'A Wonderful, Barbarous State in the Midst of Civilization': An Exploration of the Mythology of the Pariah Community.* Ph.D. Dissertation: Northeastern University.

Hofstadter, R. (1969). *Social Darwinism in American thought.* New York: George Braziller, Inc.

Holy Bible, The old and new testaments. (1868). *The Harding Royal Edition.* Philadelphia, PA: The William W. Harding Press.

Horrorbid. (2011). Interview with Tucker & Dale vs. Evil Filmmaker Eli Craig. https://www.youtube.com/watch?v=DGT37YMPJPU&list=PLkCxm2L7jC860L0 I2IDxcWO4ZpquYCiPC&index=125. Accessed on September 12, 2011.

Huth, A. H. (1875). *Marriage of Near Kin.* London: J and H. Churchill.

Investigation Discovery. (2019a). About Dead North. https://www.investigationdisco very.com/tv-shows/dead-north/about.

———. (2019b). About Homicide City. https://www.investigationdiscovery.com/tv -shows/homicide-city/about.

———. (2019c). About Murder Comes to Town. https://www.investigationdisco very.com/tv- shows/murder-comes-to-town/about.

———. (2019d). About Murder in the Heartland. https://www.investigationdisco very.com/tv-shows/murder-in-the-heartland/about.

———. (2019e). About Sugar Town. https://www.investigationdiscovery.com/tv-sho ws/sugar-town/about.

———. (2019f). About Swamp Murders. https://www.investigationdiscovery.com/tv -shows/the-wonderland-murders.

———. (2019g). About The Wonderland Murders. https://www.investigationdisco very.com/tv-shows/dead-north/about.

Isenberg, N. (2016). *White Trash: The 400-Year History of Class in America.* New York: Viking.

Jackson, S. (2017). *Dark Tales.* New York: Penguin Books.

———. (1968). *Come Along with Me.* Edited by Stanley Edgar Hyman. New York: The Viking Press.

Jicha, K. A. (2016). Portrayals of rural people and places in reality television programming: How popular cable series misrepresent rural realities. In: Fulkerson, G. M. and Thomas, A. R. Thomas (eds.), *Reimaging Rural: Urbanormative Portrayals of Rural Life,* pp. 35–57. Lanham, MD: Lexington Books.

Kaiser, S. B. and Bernstein, S. T. (2014). Rural representations in fashion and television: Co-optation and cancellation. *Fashion, Style, and Popular Culture* 1(1), 97–117.

Kermode, F. (1967). *The Sense of An Ending.* New York: Oxford University Press.

Kevles, D. J. (1985). *In the Name of Eugenics: Genetics and the Issues of Human Heredity.* Berkeley, CA: University of California Press.

Laws of the state of New Hampshire, 1867–1871.

Lawson, R. (2019). Yes, *Schitt's Creek* is Really That Good. *Vanity Fair.* https://www.vanityfair.com/hollywood/2019/01/yes-schitts-creek-really-is-that-good. Accessed on January 16, 2019.

Leonard, E. (2002). *Fire in the Hole and Other Stories.* New York, NY: William Morrow.

Levi-Strauss, C. (1969). *The Elementary Structures of Kinship.* Boston, MA: Beacon Press.

Madden, E. (2018). What's the Deal with Justin Bieber and Post Malone's White Trash Aesthetic?" https://I-d.vice.com/en_uk/article/xwkydz/whats the deal with -justin-bieber-and-post-malones-white-trash-aesthetic.

Massachusetts demographics. (2019). https://www.towncharts.com/Massachusetts/Demographics/Freetown-town-MA-Demographics-data.html.

McLennan, J. F. ([1877] 1970). *Primitive Marriage.* Edinburgh: A. C. Black.

MGDSQUAN. (2015). What are the Chances of *Wrong Turn 7* in 2016? http://www.horrorsociety.com. Accessed on May 7, 2015.

Morgan, L. H. ([1862] 1959). *The Indian Journals, 1859–1862.* Edited by White, L. Ann Arbor, MI: University of Michigan Press.

———. ([1877] 1963). *Ancient Society: Research in the Lines of Human Progress from Savagery Through Barbarism to Civilization.* Edited by Leacock, E. B. New York: The World Publishing Group.

Murphy, B. M. (2013). *The Rural Gothic in American Popular Culture: Backwoods Horror and Terror in the Wilderness.* New York: Palgrave.

Netflix. Making a Murderer. https://www.netflix.com/title/80000770.

Nye, R. A. (1985). Sociology and degeneration: The irony of progress. In: Chamberlin, J. E. and Gilman, S. (eds.), *Degeneration: The Dark Side of Progress,* pp. 49–71. New York: Columbia University Press.

O'Donnell, W. J. and Jones, D. A. (1982). *The Law of Marriage and Marriage Alternatives.* Lexington, MA: D. C. Heath and Co.

Ottenheimer, M. (1996). *Forbidden Relatives: The American Myth of Cousin Marriage.* Chicago, IL: The University of Chicago Press.

———. (1990). Lewis Henry Morgan and the prohibition of cousin marriage in the United States. *Journal of Family History* 15, 325–334.

Oxygen Network. (2019). The Piketon Family Murders. https://www.oxygen.com/the-piketon-family-murders/season-1/the-piketon-family-murders.

Parker, R. (1991). *Bodies, Pleasures, and Passions: Sexual Culture in Contemporary Brazil*. Boston, MA: Beacon Press.

Parsons, T. and Bales, R. F. (1955). *Family, Socialization, and Interaction Process*. Glencoe, IL: The Free Press.

Patrick, S. (2018). Without a paddle: Schitt's Creek, CBC, and the return to community and family in uncertain times." *Canadian Journal of Communication* 43, 297–314.

Pick, D. (1989). *Faces of Degeneration: A European Disorder, c. 1848–1918*. New York: Cambridge University Press.

Rafter, N. H. (1988). *White Trash: The Eugenic Family Studies, 1877–1919*. Boston, MA: Northeastern University Press.

Raglan, L. (1991). *Jocasta's Crime: An Anthropological Review*. New York: Howard Fertig.

Reelgood. (2020). Full List of Shows on Investigation Discovery. https://reelgood.com/tv/source/investigation_discovery_go?filter-sort=4.

Rigney, T. (2015). *Wrong Turn 7* Launches Facebook Page, Promises 2017 Release. http://www.dreadcentral.com.

Rodowick, D. N. (1984). The enemy within: The economy of violence in *The Hills Have Eyes*. In: B. Grant and C. Sharrett (eds.), *Planks of Reason: Essays on the Horror Film*, pp. 321–330. Metuchen, NJ: The Scarecrow Press.

Rogers, E. and Pridemore, W. A. (2016). Research on social disorganization theory and crime in rural communities. In: Donnermeyer, J. F. (ed.), *Routledge International Handbook of Rural Criminology*, pp. 23–31. New York: Routledge.

Roskelly, H. (1993). Telling tales out of school: A redneck daughter in the academy. In: Tokarczyk, M. and Fay, E. A. (eds.), *Working-Class Women in the Academy: Laborers in the Knowledge Factory,* pp. 292–307. Amherst, MA: University of Massachusetts Press.

Rural Sociological Society. (2015). Annual Meeting Program. http://www.ruralsociology.us/?conference=rss-2015.

Schuetz, J. (2018). Does TV Bear Some of the Responsibility for Hard Feelings Between Urban America and Small Town America? *Brookings Institute*. Retrieved at https://www.brookings.edu/blog/the-avenue/2018/02/12/does-tv-bear-some-responsibility-for-hard-feelings-between-urban-america-and-small-town-america/.

Sharrett, C. (1984). The idea of apocalypse in *The Texas Chainsaw Massacre*. In: Grant, B. K. (ed.), *Planks of Reason: Essays on the Horror Film*, pp. 255–275. Metuchen, NJ: The Scarecrow Press.

Shields, Rob. (1991). *Places on the Margin: Alternative Geographies of Modernity*. New York: Routledge.

Shilling, C. (1993). *The Body and Social Theory*. Thousand Oaks, CA: Sage.

Siegel, L. J. (2015). *Criminology: The Core*, 5th edition. Stamford, CT: Cengage Learning.

Siegel, S. (1985). Literature and degeneration: The representation of 'decadence.' In: Chamberlin, E. J. and Gilman, S. (eds.), *Degeneration: The Dark Side of Progress*, pp. 199–219. New York: Columbia University Press.

Smith, D. S. (1989). 'All in some degree related to each other': A demographic and comparative resolution of the anomaly of New England kinship. *American Historical Review* 94, 44–79.

Sommers, Z. (2017). Missing White women syndrome: An empirical analysis of race and gender disparities in online news coverage of missing persons. *The Journal of Criminal Law and Criminology* 106(2), 275–314.

Spencer, H. (1862). *First Principles of a New System of Philosophy*. New York: Appleton.

———. (1861). *Education*. London: Williams and Norgate.

State of New Hampshire, Revised Statutes, 1842.

Steel, E. (2015). Investigation Discovery Network Makes Crime Pay Off. *The New York Times*. Retrieved at https://www.nytimes.com/2015/01/05/business/media/investigation-discovery-network-makes-crime-pay.html. Accessed on January 4, 2015.

Stepan, N. (1985). Biological degeneration: Races and proper places." In: Chamberlin, J. E. and Gilman, S. (eds.), *Degeneration: The Dark Side of Progress*, pp. 97–120. New York: Columbia University Press.

Stewart, B. E. (2011). *Blood in the Hills: A History of Violence in Appalachia*. Lexington, KY: University Press of Kentucky.

Stewart, K. (1996). *A Space on the Side of the Road: Cultural Poetics in an "Other" America*. Princeton, NJ: Princeton University Press.

Stillman, S. (2007). 'The missing white girl syndrome': Disappeared women and media activism. *Gender and Development* 3, 491–502.

Sumner, C. (1994). *The Sociology of Deviance: An Obituary*. New York: Continuum.

Thomas, A., Lowe, B., Fulkerson, G. and Smith, P. (2011). *Critical Rural Theory: Structure*Space*Culture*. Lanham, MD: Lexington.

Travel Channel. (2019). Hometown Horror. https://www.travelchannel.com/shows/hometown-horror.

Trumbach, R. (1978). *The Rise of the Egalitarian Family: Aristocratic Kinship and Domestic Relations in Eighteenth-Century England*. New York: Academic Press.

Twitchell, J. B. (1987). *Forbidden Partners: The Incest Taboo in Modern Culture*. New York: Columbia University Press.

Tylor, E. B. (1878). *Researches in the Early History of Mankind and the Development of Civilization*, 3rd edition. London: John Murray.

Vernier, C. G. (1931). *American Family Laws, vol. 1*. Hartford, CT: Greenwood Press.

VideoHounds Golden Movie Retriever. (1997). New York: Visible Ink.

Walsh, B. (2013). In Town v. Country, It Turns Out That Cities are the Safest Places to Live. *Time*. Retrieved at http://science.time.com/2013/07/23/in-town-versus-country-it-turns-out-that-cities-are-the-safest-places-to-live/. Accessed on July 23, 2013.

Westbrook, P. D. (1982). *The New England Town in Fact and Fiction*. East Brunswick, NJ: Associated University Presses, Incorporated.

Williams, R. (1973). *The Country and the City*. New York: Oxford University Press.

Williams, S. (1996). "Queasy Writers: James Wong and Glen Morgan Scare Up Some Creepy X-Files." *TV Guide*, pp. 21–26.

Wolfram, Sybil. (1987). *In-Laws and Out-Laws: Kinship and Marriage in England*. New York: St. Martin's Press.

Wood, R. (1979). The American nightmare. In: Britton, A., Wood, R., and Lippe, R. (eds.), *American Nightmare: Essays on the Horror Film*, pp. 25–32. Toronto, ON: Festival of Books.

Woodrell, D. (2006). *Winter's Bone*. Boston, MA: Back Bay Books.

World Population Review. (2019). http://worldpopulationreview.com/us-cities/perryville-ky-population/.

Wray, M. and Newitz, A. (1997). *White Trash: Race and Class in America*. New York: Routledge.

Films Cited

Berlinger, J. and Sinovsky, B. (Directors). (1992). *Brother's Keeper*. American Playhouse in Association with Creative Thinking, International.

Boorman, J. (Director). (1972). *Deliverance*. United States: Warner Brothers Studio.

Craig, E. (Director). (2010). *Tucker and Dale vs. Evil*. United States: Reliance Big Pictures.

Craven, W. (Director). (1977). *The Hills Have Eyes*. United States: Blood Relations Co.

Demos, M. & Ricciardi, L. (Directors). (2015). *Making a Murderer*. Synthesis Films.

Gordon Lewis, H. (Director). (1964) *Two Thousand Maniacs!* United States: Jacqueline Kay, Inc. & Friedman-Lewis Productions.

Granik, D. (Director). (2010). *Winter's Bone*. United States: Anonymous Content.

Hershell G. L. (Director). (1964). *Two Thousand Maniacs!* United States: Jacqueline Kay, Inc. & Friedman-Lewis Productions.

Hooper, T. (Director). (1974). *The Texas Chainsaw Massacre*. United States: Vortex.

Hunt, C. (Director). 2008. Frozen River. United States: Sony Pictures.

Hurwitz, J. & Schlossberg, H. (Directors). (2008). *Harold and Kumar Escape from Guantanamo Bay*. United States: Mandate Pictures.

Kopple, B. (Director). (1976). *Harlan County, USA*. United States: Cabin Creek Films.

Lynch, J. (Director) (2007). *Wrong Turn 2: Dead End*. United States: 20th Century Fox Film Corporation.

Milev, V. (Director). (2014). *Wrong Turn 6: Last Resort*. United States: 20th Century Fox Home Entertainment.

O'Brien, D. (Director) (2009). *Wrong Turn 3: Left for Dead*. United States: 20th Century Fox Home Entertainment.

O'Brien, D. (Director). (2011). *Wrong Turn 4: Bloody Beginnings (A Prequel)*. United States: 20th Century Fox Home Entertainment.

O'Brien, D. (Director). (2012). *Wrong Turn 5: Bloodlines*. United States: 20th Century Fox Home Entertainment.

Schmidt, R. (Director). (2003). *Wrong Turn*. United States: Summit Entertainment.

Index

Italic page references indicate figures and tables.

About the Author

Karen E. Hayden is a professor in the Department of Criminology and Criminal Justice at Merrimack College. Her work has appeared in *Contemporary Sociology*, *Studies in Symbolic Interaction*, and *Teaching Sociology*. She also wrote chapters in the edited volumes, *Against Urbanormativity: Perspectives on Rural Theory* and *Reimagining Rural: Urbanormative Portrayals of Rural Life*. Karen is the author of *Society and Law* (2020). She earned her PhD in sociology from Northeastern University.